7 Financial Models for Analysts, Investors and Finance Professionals

7 Financial Models for Analysts, Investors and Finance Professionals

Theory and practical tools to help investors analyse businesses using Excel

By Paul Lower

Hh

Hh Harriman House

HARRIMAN HOUSE LTD
18 College Street
Petersfield
Hampshire
GU31 4AD
GREAT BRITAIN
Tel: +44 (0)1730 233870
Email: enquiries@harriman-house.com
Website: www.harriman-house.com

First published in Great Britain in 2019
Copyright © Paul Lower

The right of Paul Lower to be identified as the Author has been asserted in accordance
with the Copyright, Design and Patents Act 1988.

Hardback ISBN: 978-0-85719-573-9
eBook ISBN: 978-0-85719-577-7

British Library Cataloguing in Publication Data
A CIP catalogue record for this book can be obtained from the British Library.

Contents

Chapter 4 – Model 2A: Sales Forecasting   **45**

Chapter 5 – Model 2B: Cost Forecasting   **57**

About the Author

Paul Lower is a trainer, lecturer and author, specialising in financial planning and analysis, and financial modelling and forecasting. He has worked for major clients in the UK (including Associated British Foods, Reckitt Benckiser and Angel Trains) and the Middle East (including SABIC and Saudi Aramco) and has also lectured on the MBA programme at one of the UK's leading business schools.

Before moving into training he enjoyed a successful business career spanning more than 30 years. After gaining experience in blue chip companies, including Asda, H. J. Heinz and Pfizer, he held a number of Finance Director roles with major international companies in the media and publishing sector. Working for more than 20 years at board level, he gained extensive experience in financial planning and analysis, business valuations and acquisitions.

Paul is a Fellow of the Chartered Institute of Management Accountants, a Chartered Global Management Accountant and is also a Fellow of the Institute of Leadership and Management.

Acknowledgements

The job of the technical author is to write in such a way that allows readers without the same level of knowledge or experience to get a clear understanding of the topic and develop practical skills. I would like to thank Craig Pearce and his editorial team at Harriman House for their expert guidance in helping to bring clarity to my writing and offering numerous suggestions for how to improve the book.

The challenge for the financial modeller is to design an application that is user-friendly, unbreakable and bug free. This involves a time-consuming testing process and I am very grateful to my long-standing friend and business colleague, Stan Dwight, for generously giving his time to this task, as well as offering invaluable help to improve the text.

Preface

The 1970s was a decade of profound change. The oil price increase that resulted from regional conflicts in the Middle East and the formation of the Organisation of Petroleum Exporting Countries (OPEC) ushered in a period of stagnating economic growth and high levels of price inflation (stagflation), breaking what had been a sustained period of post-war prosperity in the developed economies. Another significant change in the closing years of that decade was the early-stage development of personal computers that would eventually kill off the expensive mainframe and mini computers then in use in the largest companies.

In 1978, I was working as a Management Accountant for a company that used computing technology spun-off from the US space programme to produce high-quality analysis of the seismic data coming out of the geophysical exploration for oil. I arrived at the office reception area one day to find a dozen large boxes each emblazoned with a large graphic of an apple. The finance department was allocated one of the Apple II computers that had been shipped in these boxes. The Regional CEO had ordered the machines and when we asked him what he wanted us to do with ours, he told us that he had no idea, but he expected that we would think of something. Some of the more adventurous finance team members clubbed together and bought a book on programming in BASIC (one of the earliest programming languages) and we took our first fumbling steps in using computers to do the basic numerical grunt work that was still been done by thousands of highly-trained finance professionals using rudimentary electronic calculators.

The decades that followed brought not just further extraordinary global change but also a striking increase in the rate of change. This was nowhere more obvious than in the field of personal computers and the software they used. Microsoft Excel was launched in 1985 and subsequently established itself as the de facto spreadsheet software. It had been preceded by a number of other successful products including Lotus 123 and Supercalc. From the start these spreadsheet applications revolutionised the way in which finance professionals worked and how they spent their time at the office.

Most importantly they facilitated a number of significant changes in the way that financial models could be used for business forecasting and decision-making. For example, in the 1960s Nobel Prize winning economists Modigliani and Miller had posited that the real value of a business was a function of the present value of all of the future cash flows that could be generated in perpetuity from its assets, taking into consideration the underlying risk in those assets. This principle is the basis for the business valuation model in Chapter 10. When you have had an opportunity to study the structure and functionality of this model you will have some idea of how this kind of financial modelling was all but impossible for most investment analysts and finance professionals in the age of the mainframe computer and the simple calculator. The emergence and dominance of the Shareholder Value Added (SVA) approach to business valuation during the last 25 years is due in large part to the ability to build this type of SVA financial model on a PC.

I was a working finance professional during this period and I was able to exploit much of the increasing power and functionality in these spreadsheet products to develop different financial models with which I could improve my own productivity and, more crucially, provide more meaningful insights for colleagues into the probable effects of their own business decisions and the potential impact of various kinds of risk events on company performance. This book is a guide on how to design, build and use some of the most useful of these financial models.

The book is intended primarily for investment analysts and finance professionals, who I hope will find useful practical applications for these models in their own businesses. Having had some experience as a visiting lecturer on an MBA programme, I would also imagine that the theory refresher sections, as well as the modelling sections, will be helpful to those undertaking the financial module of the MBA.

This book is in no way intended to be a 'how to' guide for those wishing to specifically advance their Excel skills. The chapters are therefore written from the starting premise that the reader already has a good working knowledge of Excel, with skills at an intermediate level.

The book is structured in ten chapters. The initial chapters are an introduction to the principles of financial modelling and provide some practical tips for using Excel to build your own financial models. The subsequent chapters deal with the each of the financial models featured in the book – in each case providing a topic refresher on the financial principles underlying the model and a detailed description of the model's design and how it operates. I've used screenshots to illustrate much of this and an Excel version of each model is available to download from the book's page on the Harriman House website (www.harriman-house.com/7finmodels).

 I would suggest that the best way to use this book is to read the topic refresher in each chapter and then move on to the financial model. Download the Excel file and explore the structure of the model and study the links between each of its sections. When you are familiar with the way in which the model operates, try changing the assumptions and see what effect this has on the key outputs from the model.

I should remind you at this point that there are only two types of financial model: those with bugs and those in which the bugs have not yet been discovered! If you adapt any of these educational models for your own use I would strongly advise that you test them exhaustively to identify any remaining bugs and, if you find any, do let me know.

Paul Lower
Spring 2019

Chapter 1

Financial Modelling and Excel Basics

Before we can look at the seven financial models in this book, some background information is needed. This chapter runs through a few separate items related to financial models and how to build them. This lays the foundations for what is to come later.

In Chapter 1, we look at why financial models are useful in the first place, how Microsoft Excel changed modelling, best practices in building models, ten tips for creating good models, and finally how to get the best results from Excel.

The need for financial models

It is an accepted business tenet that what cannot be measured cannot be managed. And many of the most critical aspects of business performance are measured financially.

Many companies, for example, define their high-level strategic goals in terms of creating and improving shareholder value. This can be measured in a number of ways based on the key drivers of financial performance: profit, cash flow, capital invested and asset management efficiency. Other financial measures deal with financial strength, financial structure and risk.

Effective financial management and decision-making in any business therefore relies on analysis of past results and forecasts of future performance. These are areas in which financial models can provide powerful tools to automate and accelerate what were previously manual calculation tasks that absorbed considerable amounts of time that can now be better spent on interpreting the output from financial models.

Financial models – what they are and how they are used most effectively

A model is something designed to be a replica of something else; a model aims to reproduce the key attributes of the object on which it is based, often to facilitate an easier analysis of its key features. For example, a computer-generated architectural model provides the opportunity to assess the important attributes of a proposed design without the need to actually build it.

Financial models provide an abstract representation of financial situations for different scenarios. They can, for example, provide a simulation of the relationship between the drivers of revenue and costs for the purposes of a business valuation. In other applications they can be used to test the benefit of a portfolio of different kinds of security, or test the costs, risks and financial return of a planned capital investment project.

Financial models can be used in a wide range of different situations. The development and evolution of sophisticated spreadsheet software tools like Microsoft Excel provides the basis for using *key driver* models that can rapidly simulate a large number of scenarios to assist in financial decision-making and risk management. In this book, I provide seven of these key driver models.

Using Excel spreadsheet software for financial modelling

Excel is now the de facto spreadsheet application. Over the course of the last 30 years, it has revolutionised the way in which financial data is analysed and business and investment decisions are made.

For example, the way in which finance professionals value businesses has been transformed by the use of spreadsheet software. Shareholder value analysis has become one of the standard tools for business valuation, based on the discounted value of a company's projected future cash flows. But although the approach was first mooted in the 1960s, it was not until the advent of Lotus 123, and Microsoft Excel, that investment analysts were able to build financial models to forecast business cash flows and easily test the sensitivity of their valuations against the impact of various types of risks.

Best practice in building financial models

Financial models, whether they are developed with Excel, or some other application, have the following key attributes:

- **Structure**: Input assumptions are used to make all of the necessary calculations and to generate the model's output. The input and output parts of the model are separated.

- **Consistency**: In their structure, layout and organisation.

- **Flexibility**: Rather than using one definitive set of data for its assumptions, a financial model allows all of the assumptions to be easily changed.

- **They are dynamic**: When any of the input assumptions are changed the output automatically changes; so rather than providing a static report, a model provides a flexible and powerful tool with which to assess the effect of changes in the assumptions.

- **They exploit causal relationships**: When the value of one model variable has a strong causal link with another, this is exploited to connect the inputs with the outputs in a more realistic way. For example, a model to value a petrochemical company might link a number of calculations to the market price of crude oil, a key factor affecting the cost of raw materials.

- **Transparency**: They use simple and clear formulae that can be easily understood.

- **Accuracy**: Without over complication or unnecessary detail.

Ten steps to create good financial models

Time pressures and deadlines, and the power of spreadsheet tools, all make it very tempting to jump straight in and start building a financial model. But hard experience shows that hastily-built financial models will invariably reveal their bugs and design weaknesses at the moment of maximum potential embarrassment – when making a presentation to the investment committee, for example.

The following steps will produce a financial model that not only gives required answers but, when all relevant key business drivers and causal relationships have been identified, will provide invaluable insights into the key factors affecting the answer and how sensitive these factors are to the effects of risk and uncertainty.

1. **Identify users**: Will you be the sole user, or will others also use your financial model? Do the other users have financial skills? What will they want to achieve from the model?

2. **Define purpose**: What is the purpose of the model, what will it be used for, what are the users trying to determine? Different users may place a different emphasis on different elements of the model.

3. **Specify outputs**: It may seem more logical to start by focusing on the model inputs, but the most efficient way to build a financial model is to start by identifying the desired output. This will make it easier to work through the required calculation processes to identify the inputs and data needed.

4. **Specify calculations**: What kind of calculations will be required to produce the output data? What kind of causal relationships can be established and used in calculations to produce the data required?

5. **Specify inputs**: What kind of raw data will be required from external sources, as well as from historical data sources within the organisation? What are the assumptions that will be needed; which are the key drivers that really influence the output from the model?

6. **Design**: How should the model be structured? Which are the appropriate spreadsheet functions and formulae to convert the inputs into the specified outputs? A model that is well thought out, carefully structured and designed can make the difference

between creating a powerful decision-making tool or a model that is difficult to understand and use, that produces incorrect, inconsistent or unclear results.

7. **Map**: With larger and more complex models it may be helpful to first use simple flowcharting tools to produce a map of exactly how the model will work in terms of inputs, processes and functions, and outputs.

8. **Build**: The model can now be built, based on a clear specification and a mapped design. Investment in the earlier steps ought to make the building process relatively straightforward. If the model is to be shared with other users, it is good practice to protect and lock the calculations and outputs. The input cells should, of course, be left unprotected, to enable the user to make use of the model.

9. **Document**: A good financial model should be documented to describe the source of the data required, how the model works, and where to find and how to interpret the key output data and results. This is particularly important if the model is to be used by others who did not design it. It is helpful to put the documentation on the first sheet of the workbook.

10. **Test**: The unwritten rule of financial modelling is that there are two types of model: those that have bugs, and those where the bugs haven't been found. Bugs may not be obvious when the model is being built and the job at the testing stage is to use different assumptions and scenarios with the specific aim of flushing out any problems. It can be helpful to give the model to a colleague to experiment with; it is quite possible they will attempt to use the model in a way that you, as the designer, might not. Until the bugs have been identified they can't be fixed. Time spent testing is time well invested.

Tips on how to get the best results using Excel for financial modelling

Excel is an incredibly powerful and flexible spreadsheet software tool, but in its strength also lies its weakness: the almost limitless options for writing functions and formatting reports can make it very hard to produce consistent models, difficult to understand how a model is supposed to work and time consuming to de-bug. The following tips will help you to avoid the pitfalls and produce reliable models:

- **Standard approach**: Develop a standard approach for building Excel models.

- **Work collaboratively with colleagues**: Share ownership and subject new workbooks to team review and testing.

- **Always consider the user and audience**: If the model is solely for use by you and your team, a shared understanding might allow you to reduce the amount of documentation and reduce the necessity for sheet and cell protection. If the workbook is for use by non-financial users outside the department, care will be needed with documentation and protection.

- **Aim for simplicity**: Although it is tempting to use the power of Excel to deploy complex nested formulae, for example, to build a very concise spreadsheet, consider those who will use your model and aim for efficient simplicity rather than complexity, particularly in formulae design.

- **Allow for expansion and development**: Make sure that formulae are written so that rows and columns can be easily inserted without correcting formulae.

- **Build in check totals**: If a total is derived from rows, run a check total based on columns and compare. This can be hidden and any differences reported as an error message, if necessary.

- **Always avoid hard-coding values**: For the model to be dynamic you will need to ensure that all calculated values in the model are derived from the separate assumptions, or are totals of other numbers that are.

- **Separate input data worksheets from reporting sheets**: Have one sheet for collecting data and data input. Use separate sheets for reporting data and make sure they are protected.

- **Keep the colour scheme and format simple**: This will draw attention to the important parts of a spreadsheet. Keep your formatting style consistent as well. For example, input cells are often blue.

- **Don't merge cells**: Merged cells can cause some formulae to generate odd results, and cause havoc with sorting and filtering.

- **Document workbooks**: Make sure that anybody using your workbook will be able to understand its purpose, structure and operation. Include a list of defined names in use in the workbook, and their purpose.

- **Be wary of using macros**: Even simple recording macros can be confusing for unsophisticated users; complicated VBA macros can be impenetrable, even for experienced users with a little knowledge of VBA. If you must use macros, make sure they are very thoroughly documented.

- **Use IFERROR to avoid erroneous error messages**: A common example is the #DIV/0! error that appears if a formula results from a number being divided by zero; this commonly happens when using percentage calculations for a column of numbers. This kind of error can confuse unsophisticated users and undermine confidence in your workbook. IFERROR can replace the error message with a blank space or zero.

- **Rigorously test your workbook**: Before you circulate reports based on your new spreadsheet, or before you issue it to others to use for their own work, make sure that you have tested all aspects of the spreadsheet's functionality and its calculations.

The seven models described in this book and the process for building them will follow all of the best practice steps for creating good models in Excel that I have just outlined. By following this guide, you will be putting these steps to work.

Chapter 2

Understanding and Using Financial Statements

Understanding financial statements

Financial statements are the source of much of the information needed for financial analysis and financial modelling. In many cases, they may provide a suitable framework on which to base the structure of a financial model. This chapter is a topic refresher on the information provided by each of the financial statements, their structure, and how they are related. If you are completely conversant with financial statements you can skip this chapter.

The purpose of financial statements

The purpose of financial statements is to provide users with information about the financial performance of a business, its financial position and changes in its financial position from one period to the next. This information can be used to assess the firm's ability to generate cash, and the timing and certainty of this cash generation. The ability to generate cash is fundamental to the survival and health of a company and determines, amongst other things, whether it will be able to pay its lenders, suppliers and employees. Financial statements also provide a way of making the directors accountable to the shareholders for the way they have managed the business and the results they have achieved.

Financial position

The firm's financial resources, its financial structure and its solvency and liquidity status all affect the financial position of the business. Information about the financial resources the company controls, and its track record of managing these resources, is useful in forming a view of its ability to generate strong cash flows in the future.

Information about financial structure – its combination of debt and share capital – is useful for predicting the firm's future borrowing needs.

Information about changes in the company's financial position is useful for assessing its investing, financing and operating activities during the period, and its need for, and ability to generate, cash.

Financial performance

Information about the firm's financial performance, particularly profitability, is useful for assessing its future profitability, potential changes in the resources it might have in the future and how effectively it might use any additional resources.

Some key accounting concepts

The concepts and rules applied in preparing financial statements shape the way that some important things are measured and presented. These concepts mean that financial statements are very helpful in some respects, like presenting a cautious view of the company's resources and its ability to meet its liabilities. In other respects, the concepts place serious constraints on the way in which financial statements can present a fair view of the market value of the enterprise.

Accruals concept

Financial statements are prepared based on the accruals concept. This means that the effect of financial transactions are recognised in financial statements in the period in which they take place and not in the period when the cash flows relating to those transactions occur. This means that revenue is recognised in the period in which the revenue is earned or invoiced to the customer. Also, expenses are recognised in the period in which they are incurred and are matched to the revenue-generating activity to which they relate.

Prudence concept

Financial statements may not include any profits that have not been realised in the form of cash or another form of asset like a receivable. It also means that provision should be made in financial statements for all known losses, even if the amount and timing is uncertain. In cases where amount and timing is uncertain, a prudent estimate must be made. The concept does not permit the use of hidden reserves for the purpose of profit smoothing.

Going concern concept

Financial statements are prepared on the assumption that the firm can continue to operate for the foreseeable future and is not expected to go into liquidation. This is relevant for the valuation of the firm's assets. When all of a company's assets are sold under the pressure of a liquidation, they often fail to make true market value. The prudence concept means that any expected reduction in asset value would have to be reflected in the value in the financial statements.

Consistency concept

This requires companies to adopt the same treatment of similar items from one accounting period to the next. The company must disclose all changes in the accounting treatment of any items and restate the comparative figure for the previous accounting period.

The structure of financial statements

In every actively trading firm there is a continuous stream of business events, the volume and velocity of which will depend on the nature and size of the enterprise. This is illustrated in Figure 2.1.

Figure 2.1: Stream of business events

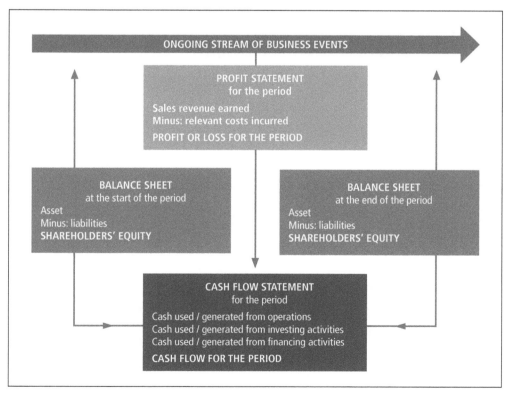

The three basic financial statements explained below are based on the information from this stream of business events.

1. Balance sheet – statement of financial position

At any point in this stream of events, a snapshot may be taken of the company's financial position. This snapshot is represented by a balance sheet. Another snapshot taken at any point further along the stream of business transactions will, of course, show a different snapshot of the company's financial position.

Each balance sheet shows the company's assets (what it owns), minus its liabilities (what it owes) and the resulting residual value in the business, referred to as the shareholders' equity. The relationship between these three elements is constant and represented by the accounting equation:

$$Assets - liabilities = shareholders'\ equity$$

An example balance sheet from fictional company ACME Trading Company Ltd is shown below.

ACME TRADING COMPANY LIMITED

Balance sheet as at 31st December

$000's omitted	2015	2014
Non-current assets		
Property, plant and equipment	33,700	34,800
	33,700	34,800
Current assets		
Stock	41,795	36,580
Trade debtors	24,658	22,630
Cash and cash equivalents	236	73
	66,689	59,283
Current liabilities		
Trade and other creditors	(6,765)	(6,013)
Borrowings	(4,640)	(4,640)
Current tax liabilities	(1,080)	(1,353)
	(12,485)	(12,006)
Net current assets	54,204	47,277
Non-current liabilities		
Borrowings	(4,029)	(8,019)
NET ASSETS	**83,875**	**74,058**
Share capital	30,000	30,000
Retained earnings	53,875	44,058
SHAREHOLDERS' EQUITY	**83,875**	**74,058**

Companies may adopt one of several formats for presenting their balance sheets but they will usually show the same elements as the vertical style presentation above. Let's look at each of these elements in turn.

Assets

Non-current, or **fixed assets**, are those things the company owns that are used in the business to carry on its trade. Property, plant and equipment are examples of physical, or tangible, assets. Brands and patents are examples of intangible assets. When non-current assets are first purchased they are shown in the balance sheet at cost and in each subsequent accounting period the balance sheet value is reduced to reflect the fact that fixed assets wear out. This means that the balance sheet value of fixed assets may sometimes be significantly less than their replacement cost or market value. Some companies may revalue their assets from time to time if the balance sheet value is less than the fair market value of the assets.

Cash, and other assets, like stock (inventory) and debtors, that are expected to be converted back to cash within 12 months, are shown as **current assets**. Firms that make and sell, or buy and sell, products may invest a significant amount of cash into stocks of raw materials, partially completed stock and finished stock. When the stock is sold on credit terms it is converted into trade debtors and then, when the customers have paid, debtors are converted back into cash, ready to be invested again in inventory. This process is referred to as the trade cycle.

Liabilities

Current liabilities include amounts the company owes that must be paid within 12 months – they usually include payments owed to suppliers, the tax authorities and, if the company has borrowings that must be repaid within the next 12 months, this will also be shown in current liabilities.

Any borrowing and other types of debt payable after 12 months are shown as **non-current liabilities**. The company may also make provision for other types of liabilities that they believe may arise. For example, possible legal claims.

Liabilities are important because the survival of any business depends on its ability to cover both its short-term and long-term financial obligations. The amount of debt in the company, the proportion of debt to equity and the company's ability to pay the interest on its debt, will all have a direct impact on any assessment of the financial strength of the business and the willingness of banks, or other institutions, to lend money to the business.

Balance sheet limitations

The accounting concepts and rules applied in preparing financial statements impose limitations on the way in which information about the firm's financial position may be presented. This must be considered when analysing and interpreting financial statements. For example, valuable brands may be built up over many years by investment in marketing and advertising, but accounting rules require marketing costs to be treated as period costs, rather than assets, and deducted from sales revenue to calculate profit. For this reason some of the most valuable global brands that have been built by years of marketing do not appear as assets on the firm's balance sheet.

Financial statements are always prepared on a prudent basis, so profits may only be recognised when they have been realised as cash, or some other kind of asset. Assets may only be recognised in the balance sheet when their cost may be reliably determined. This means that intangible assets (like brands, customer relationships and human talent) may not be included in balance sheet. Intangibles represent a significant proportion of the market value of modern companies like Google and Facebook, leading to a significant disparity between the balance sheet value and market value of the company's assets.

2. The income statement or profit statement

The income statement measures the profit, or loss, generated from the business transactions during the period between the opening and closing balance sheet. The profit, or loss, is calculated by deducting the costs incurred from the sales revenue earned in this period.

An example income statement from ACME Trading Company Ltd is shown below.

ACME TRADING COMPANY LIMITED

Income statement for year ending 31st December

$000's omitted	2015	2014
Sales	120,000	118,000
Cost of goods sold	(77,160)	(73,160)
Gross profit	42,840	44,840
Administrative expenses	(29,100)	(27,600)
Operating profit	**13,740**	**17,240**
Finance costs	(650)	(840)
Profit before tax	13,090	16,400
Taxation	(3,273)	(4,100)
PROFIT AFTER TAX	**9,817**	**12,300**

The end result at the bottom of the income statement is profit, or loss.

Profit is a measure of the value created for shareholders; it may be distributed to shareholders in cash, as a dividend, or retained by the company as part of shareholders' equity.

It is important to understand that profit and cash flow measure different things.

Profit and cash flow measure different things

Profit is calculated based on sales invoiced to customers and the costs incurred in generating that revenue, rather than actual receipts and payments of cash. Profit is calculated after an accounting charge for the depreciation of the business assets that wear out over their useful lives. However, depreciation has no impact on cash flow.

3. Cash flow statement

Cash flow measures changes in the company's cash balances as a result of the trading activities, investment activities, and financing activities during the period. Cash flow takes into account many items that are not considered in calculating profit. For example, share capital issued, bank borrowings and repayments.

An example cash flow statement from ACME Trading Company Ltd is shown below.

ACME TRADING COMPANY LIMITED

Cash flow statement for year ending 31st December

$000's omitted	2015	2014
Operating profit	13,740	17,240
Depreciation	3,600	3,600
EBITDA	17,340	20,840
(Increase)/decrease in stocks	(5,215)	(7,000)
(Increase)/decrease in debtors	(2,028)	(4,466)
(Decrease)/increase in creditors	752	983
(Increase)/decrease in working capital	(6,491)	(10,483)
Corporation tax paid	(3,546)	(3,861)
Net cash generated from operating activities	**7,303**	**6,496**
Purchase of plant and equipment	(2,500)	(2,500)
Net cash used in investing activities	**(2,500)**	**(2,500)**
Repayment of borrowings	(4,640)	(4,640)
Net cash used in financing activities	**(4,640)**	**(4,640)**
NET CHANGE IN CASH AND CASH EQUIVALENTS	**163**	**(644)**

Comparing financials for different companies

Investors may find it helpful to compare the financial statements of different companies as a means of identifying those that are better managed and deliver better results. Managers may also find it useful to benchmark their own company's results against a competitor to identify possible areas for business improvement. But there are a number of potential difficulties in making a direct comparison based purely on financial statements and some adjustments may need to be made in order to make a direct comparison, for example:

- There can be significant differences in the preparation of financial statements between companies following US accounting practices, firms using the International Accounting Standards Board (IASB) framework, and other foreign companies using national accounting rules.

- Directors choose their company's own accounting policies that deal with the treatment of matters like depreciation and inventory valuation. There may be material differences between the accounting policies of two companies.

- There may be differences in the way that brands and other intangible assets are treated in the financial statements. Purchased intangible assets are shown on the balance sheet at cost, subject to periodic review against fair market value and, if necessary, reduced in value. On the other hand, intangible assets that have been internally generated by the business will generally not have any value assigned to them in that company's balance sheet.

Chapter 3

Model 1: Key Financial Indicators

Published financial statements are primarily designed to meet the external reporting requirements imposed by the regulatory authorities in the country in which the company's shares are listed and traded on a stock exchange.

A great deal of information is presented in a listed company's financial report. The BP 2016 financial report, for example, runs to more than 100 pages of financial statements and notes. However, this information is still insufficient to make a complete assessment of the financial performance and financial strength of the business.

Financial analysis is a way of finding out more about a company's performance over a sustained period – both in the financial markets where it competes for investors, and in the customer markets where it competes to sell its products and services. To achieve and maintain success a business must perform well in both of these areas.

Financial analysis focuses attention on where changes are taking place. Although it cannot provide all of the answers, it helps to raise the right questions which, when answered, will help to form a comprehensive picture of the performance and strength of the firm.

Therefore, the first model we are going to look at is the Key Financial Indicators model. Using this model, we will be able to construct a database using the key financial data from financial statements that will be used to calculate a set of financial ratios. Once the database has been constructed and the formulae for the ratios have been entered, it will be relatively easy to add new data to the database and to copy the ratio formulae each time a new set of financial results becomes available for the company under analysis. This automates the financial analysis process to a large extent and allows the user to focus on the interpretation of the analysis provided by the model.

I have used Associated British Foods Plc (ABF) to illustrate the construction and use of the Financial Indicator Model. ABF is a diversified international food, ingredients and retail group, it is a FTSE 100 company and owns a number of well-known UK brands, including Primark. Its annual reports are available online.

The Financial Indicator Model

- **Users:** A financial analyst, or investment analyst, would typically use this tool to automate the financial analysis process.

- **Purpose:** To calculate a range of comparative financial indicators on which to base a comprehensive view of the financial performance and financial strength of a company. The model also highlights areas for management attention to improve financial performance and shareholder value.

- **Outputs:** Summary overview of five years' key numbers; vertical and horizontal analysis of key numbers from the income statement and balance sheet; financial ratios for profitability, working capital efficiency, liquidity, capital structure, shareholder returns and cash flow.

- **Calculations:** Basic functions to calculate percentages and financial ratios.

- **Inputs:** Readily available information from financial statements published in an annual report, and selected information from Bloomberg.com.

- **Design:** The INPUT sheet consists of a database of financial data extracted from published financial statements and some additional information from Bloomberg.com. Four calculation and output sheets comprise:

  - OVERVIEW

  - INCOME STATEMENT ANALYSIS

  - BALANCE SHEET ANALYSIS

  - FINANCIAL RATIOS

The section below includes screenshots from the Financial Indicator Model. Please refer to the Excel workbook: 'FINANCIAL INDICATOR MODEL – ABF PLC.xlsx' to see the formulae used in each of the examples given.

Topic refresher – the financial analysis toolkit

Before we can look in detail at the construction of the Financial Indicator Model, we first need a topic refresher on the financial analyst's toolkit and the purpose of the various classes of ratios that are used in the model. When I analyse a company's financials for the first time I take a step-by-step systematic approach to build up a detailed picture of the firm's financial performance and financial strength. I start by preparing an overview of some of the most important numbers and how they have developed over a number of years. I then work my way through the calculation of the different classes of financial ratios described below.

Financial analysis is about building on the picture presented by the financial statements. Most of the data required for the calculations in the model are available from these statements and the notes accompanying them. The closing share prices used here were taken from Bloomberg.com, and this kind of information is also available from Yahoo

Finance or the FT website. All of the data required for the output are entered to the input database sheet – the calculation/output sheets take all of their data from this input sheet.

The table below shows the financial data required for the model's database that is used as the input for the financial analysis model.

ASSOCIATED BRITISH FOODS PLC						
£m's omitted		**2015**	**2014**	**2013**	**2012**	**2011**
Sales revenue		12,800	12,943	13,315	12,252	11,065
Cost of sales [1]		9,771	9,793	10,095	9,292	8,347
Operating profit		947	1,080	1,093	873	842
Finance expense		61	73	100	114	101
Profit attributable to equity shareholders		532	762	591	555	541
Non-current assets		6,423	6,846	6,921	6,971	7,039
Inventories		1,827	1,631	1,581	1,500	1,425
Trade debtors		1,176	1,293	1,342	1,236	1,259
Cash and cash equivalents		702	519	362	391	341
Other current assets		144	183	139	142	138
Current portion of loans and overdrafts		319	358	394	538	729
Trade payables		2,226	2,046	1,881	1,752	1,627
Other current liabilities		197	280	251	298	186
Long term portion of loans		577	607	772	914	897
Equity attributable to equity shareholders		6,336	6,437	6,133	5,834	5,748
Net cash flow from operating activities		1,166	1,439	1,276	1,240	736
		2015	**2014**	**2013**	**2012**	**2011**
Closing share price [2]	Pence	3053.3	2,564.9	1,747.1	1,224.8	1,036.3
Diluted earnings per share	Pence	67.3	96.5	74.8	70.3	68.7
Dividend per share	Pence	35.0	34.0	32.0	28.5	24.8
Shares outstanding	Millions	790	790	790	789	788

1 Information taken from Note 2 to the financial statements
2 Information taken from Bloomberg.com: nearest to balance sheet date

Five-year summary overview

The first step is to produce an overview summary, extracting selected items from the financial statements, as shown in the table below. This summary is a good way to present some of the key financial indicators on one sheet. It is by no means a comprehensive picture, but it quickly provides a broad picture of how the company has performed.

ASSOCIATED BRITISH FOODS PLC		OVERVIEW OF FINANCIAL RESULTS				
		2015	2014	2013	2012	2011
Sales revenue	£m	12,800	12,943	13,315	12,252	11,065
Operating profit	£m	947	1,080	1,093	873	842
Profit attributable to equity shareholders	£m	532	762	591	555	541
Net assets	£m	7,849	8,146	8,213	8,190	8,389
Return on net assets		12.1%	13.3%	13.3%	10.7%	10.0%
Debt ratio		11.4%	11.8%	14.2%	17.7%	19.4%
Closing share price	Pence	3053.3	2564.9	1747.1	1224.8	1036.3
Earnings per share	Pence	67.3	96.5	74.8	70.3	68.7
Dividend per share	Pence	35.0	34.0	32.0	28.5	24.8
Operating cash flow per share	Pence	147.6	182.2	161.5	157.2	93.4

Income statement analysis

Two simple techniques are used to aid comparison of key financial indicators and to identify trends in the five-year financial data. Vertical analysis, or common sizing, expresses various financial indicators as a percentage of a base figure, usually sales revenue, as in the example below. You can see the vertical analysis in the '% of sales revenue' section of the table. This allows the ABF numbers to be compared on a like-for-like basis: it shows that not only has operating profit reduced in 2015 because of lower sales revenue, but the rate at which profit is being generated is also lower, explained to some extent by the lower rate of gross profit.

Horizontal analysis, or trend analysis, calculates the percentage change in each of the key indicators from one year to the next, making it easier to identify trends in the data over the period. This can be seen in the '% change over previous year' section of the table. Horizontal analysis makes it easy to compare changes in ABF sales revenue with gross profit and operating profit.

ASSOCIATED BRITISH FOODS PLC	INCOME STATEMENT ANALYSIS				
£m's omitted	2015	2014	2013	2012	2011
Sales revenue	12,800	12,943	13,315	12,252	11,065
Gross profit	3,029	3,150	3,220	2,960	2,718
Operating profit	947	1,080	1,093	873	842
Profit attributable to equity shareholders	532	762	591	555	541
% of sales revenue					
Gross profit	23.7%	24.3%	24.2%	24.2%	24.6%
Operating profit	7.4%	8.3%	8.2%	7.1%	7.6%
Profit attributable to equity shareholders	4.2%	5.9%	4.4%	4.5%	4.9%
% change over previous year					
Sales revenue	(1.1)%	(2.8)%	8.7%	10.7%	
Gross profit	(3.8)%	(2.2)%	8.8%	8.9%	
Operating profit	(12.3)%	(1.2)%	25.2%	3.7%	
Profit attributable to equity shareholders	(30.2)%	28.9%	6.5%	2.6%	

Balance sheet analysis

Common sizing can also be applied to the key balance sheet numbers, as shown in the following table.

ASSOCIATED BRITISH FOODS PLC	BALANCE SHEET ANALYSIS				
£m's omitted	2015	2014	2013	2012	2011
Net assets [1]	7,849	8,146	8,213	8,190	8,389
Non-current assets	6,423	6,846	6,921	6,971	7,039
Current assets	3,849	3,626	3,424	3,269	3,163
Current liabilities excluding bank loans	2,423	2,326	2,132	2,050	1,813
Net working capital	1,426	1,300	1,292	1,219	1,350
Debt	896	965	1,166	1,452	1,626
% of net assets					
Non-current assets	81.8%	84.0%	84.3%	85.1%	83.9%
Current assets	49.0%	44.5%	41.7%	39.9%	37.7%
Current liabilities excluding bank loans	30.9%	28.6%	26.0%	25.0%	21.6%
Net working capital	18.2%	16.0%	15.7%	14.9%	16.1%
Debt	11.4%	11.8%	14.2%	17.7%	19.4%

1 Net assets = non-current assets + net working capital (net current assets excluding current portion of bank loans)

Ratio analysis

Ratios use the relationship between one financial indicator and another to provide greater insight into financial performance and strength. Ratios also allow easier comparison from one year to another, and from one company to another. Different groups of ratios focus on various aspects of performance and strength.

I run through some different groups of ratios below.

Return on investment (ROI)

ROI is a fundamental finance concept. Investors' funds are attracted by the best rate of return, but different investments carry different risks, so the return must reflect the level of risk taken. The relationship between risk and return is represented in Figure 3.1.

Figure 3.1

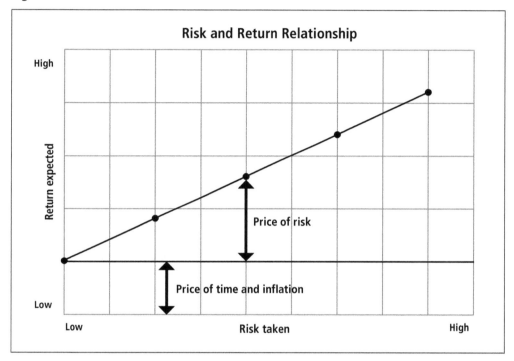

The greater level of risk that the investor perceives is being taken, the greater level of return that will be sought. But even when no risk is perceived, the investor will still seek a return because cash received in the future is considered to have less value than cash received today. This so-called *time value of money* represents the loss of other spending and investment opportunities. Investors may also expect an additional return during periods of inflation.

Profitability ratios

Value is created for shareholders when the return on the capital invested in the business is greater than the cost of providing that capital. There are a number of profitability ratios that express the profit generated by the company as a return on the different kinds of capital invested in the business.

The table below shows three key profitability ratios for ABF. These ratios, and the relationship between them, are explained in the section below.

ASSOCIATED BRITISH FOODS PLC	RATIO ANALYSIS				
	2015	2014	2013	2012	2011
Profitability ratios					
Return on net assets [1]	12.1%	13.3%	13.3%	10.7%	10.0%
Profit margin	7.4%	8.3%	8.2%	7.1%	7.6%
Net asset turnover	1.63	1.59	1.62	1.50	1.32

1 Net assets = non-current assets + net working capital (net current assets excluding current portion of bank loans)

Return on net assets (RONA)

RONA measures ROI by expressing the operating profit before interest charges and taxation as a percentage of the company's net assets. Firms are usually financed by a combination of shareholders' capital and debt capital, comprising bank loans, capital leases and corporate bonds. Capital is invested in the net assets of the business in the form of non-current (fixed) assets and net working capital (cash, inventory and trade credit). RONA is a good measure of how effectively the firm manages its net assets. It is not affected by the way in which the business is funded, which makes it a good ratio for comparison with prior years and with other businesses. RONA is calculated as:

$$Return\ on\ net\ assets\ = \frac{Operating\ profit}{Net\ assets} \times 100$$

Net assets can be calculated as:

$$Non-current\ assets + current\ assets - current\ liabilities$$

If the company has interest bearing debt capital due for repayment within 12 months of the balance sheet date, this will be included in current liabilities. This current portion of long-term debt does not form part of working capital and should be excluded from current liabilities for the purpose of calculating net assets. This adjustment has been made in the ABF case study.

Two other ratios give a useful insight into the levers affecting RONA: profit margin and net asset turnover. The relationship between these ratios is such that:

$$Return\ on\ net\ assets\ =\ Profit\ margin\ \times\ Net\ asset\ turnover$$

Profit margin

Profit margin calculates the rate at which a business generates profit on its sales.

$$Profit\ margin\ =\ \frac{Operating\ profit}{Sales\ revenue}\ \times\ 100$$

Net asset turnover

Net asset turnover reflects the capital investment needed in an industry sector to be able to compete and generate sales revenue. It is also an indicator of how effectively the firm manages its assets.

$$Net\ asset\ turnover\ =\ \frac{Sales\ revenue}{Net\ assets}$$

Profit margin and asset turnover can vary quite dramatically between different industry sectors because of differences in cost structure, competition factors and other factors. But significant changes in one company's profit margin or net asset turnover from one year to another would require further analysis and explanation.

RONA ratios are sometimes based on average net asset investment in the financial year in question. For simplicity, the model calculates net assets based on the closing balance sheet. Either method is acceptable. More importantly, a consistent approach should be used for comparison with prior years and other companies.

Efficiency and working capital ratios

Two further ratios provide a deeper insight into the factors driving net asset turnover performance. These are fixed asset turnover and working capital turnover.

The table below shows six of the financial ratios that provide further information and insight into the efficiency with which the company manages its assets.

ASSOCIATED BRITISH FOODS PLC	RATIO ANALYSIS				
	2015	2014	2013	2012	2011
Asset efficiency ratios					
Fixed asset turnover	2.0	1.9	1.9	1.8	1.6
Working capital turnover	9.0	10.0	10.3	10.1	8.2
Days sales in inventory	68	61	57	59	62
Days sales outstanding	34	36	37	37	42
Creditor days	83	76	68	69	71
Working capital cycle	19	21	26	27	33

Fixed asset turnover

This ratio measures how well the company makes use of its non-current assets.

$$Fixed\ asset\ turnover = \frac{Sales\ revenue}{Fixed\ assets}$$

Working capital turnover

Working capital turnover measures how well working capital is being managed.

$$Working\ capital\ turnover = \frac{Sales\ revenue}{Current\ assets\ -\ current\ liabilities}$$

Working capital efficiency

Working capital efficiency ratios measure how well the company manages its receivables, inventory and trade payables. They can also indicate whether the company has too much or too little invested in working capital. When too much is invested in working capital, net asset turnover will reduce and, as a result, the return on net assets will be lower. But under-investment in working capital can be an indication of liquidity problems – when working capital is low in comparison with the industry average, this might indicate that current assets are being financed to an excessive extent by trade credit.

Days' sales in inventory (DSI)

This is a good measure of inventory management efficiency, showing on average how long it will take to sell the stock on hand. There is no *correct* figure, but it can provide a useful insight to compare the figure to previous years and other companies in the same industry sector.

$$Days\ sales\ in\ inventory\ = \frac{Inventory\ at\ cost}{Cost\ of\ sales} \times 365$$

Days' sales outstanding (DSO)

This is a measure of how long the company takes to collect cash from its customers. Standard trade credit terms vary from one industry sector to another and there are also differences between different international regions.

$$Days\ sales\ outstanding\ = \frac{Trade\ debtors}{Sales\ revenue} \times 365$$

Days' purchases outstanding (DPO)

This is a similar measure to DSO and it gives an insight into whether a business is taking full advantage of, or perhaps straining, trade credit available from suppliers.

$$Days\ purchases\ outstanding\ = \frac{Trade\ creditors}{Cost\ of\ sales} \times 365$$

The working capital cycle

Together these factors will determine the length of the cash operating cycle or working capital cycle that measures the average length of time it takes from receiving a customer order to receiving cash from customers in settlement.

Working capital cycle	days
Average inventory turnover period	X
+ Average time for customers to pay	X
- Average credit period from suppliers	(X)
= Working capital cycle	X

How financial indicators guide improvements in ROI

Figure 3.2

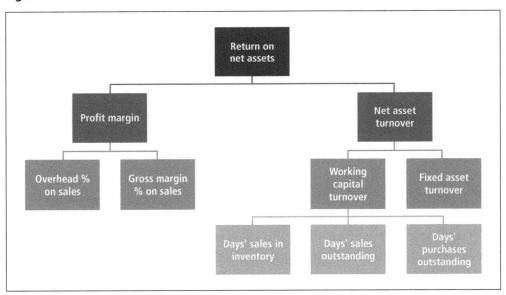

The pyramid of ratios in Figure 3.2 illustrates how the various important financial drivers affect return on investment (ROI). The pyramid shows how improvements in the ratios driving profit margin and net asset turnover can improve profitability and ROI. For example, any reductions that can be achieved in inventory and debtor levels without affecting customer service and competitiveness will improve cash flow and increase cash reserves. Any surplus cash may be used to pay dividends and the effect of this will be to reduce net asset value (and at the same time, shareholders' equity) and improve RONA.

Alternatively, the surplus funds may be used to finance product innovation and development that can, over a somewhat longer period, lead to higher product sales, improving profit and ROI. Similarly, improvements in gross profit and reductions in overhead expenses will also produce an improvement in profit margin that would increase RONA.

Liquidity ratios

Liquidity ratios deal with the company's abilities to meet its short-term liabilities. There are two measures of liquidity: current ratio and acid test ratio.

The table below shows the two financial ratios commonly used to measure the company's liquidity.

ASSOCIATED BRITISH FOODS PLC	RATIO ANALYSIS				
	2015	2014	2013	2012	2011
Liquidity ratios					
Current ratio	1.40	1.35	1.36	1.26	1.24
Acid test ratio	0.74	0.74	0.73	0.68	0.68

Current ratio

The current ratio measures the extent to which the cash, and other assets that can be converted back into cash within 12 months, cover the debts that will fall due for payment within 12 months. When calculating liquidity ratios the portion of long-term debt repayable within 12 months of the balance sheet date is included as part of current liabilities.

$$Current\ ratio\ = \frac{Current\ assets}{Current\ liabilities}$$

Acid test ratio

The acid test ratio takes into account only those assets that can be quickly converted into cash, so inventories are ignored in this calculation.

$$Acid\ test\ ratio\ = \frac{Cash + debtors}{Current\ liabilities}$$

As a general rule, the company's current assets are expected to be at least equal, or greater, than its current liabilities. But in some industry sectors it is common to find that the acid test ratio is less than 1. For example, an acid test ratio of 0.6 is not uncommon in the supermarket sector, where customers pay in cash and suppliers extend long trade credit terms. These businesses are highly cash generative and there is usually no significant risk that they will be unable to pay their debts as they fall due (the legal test of insolvency).

Excessively high liquidity ratios may indicate that the firm is inefficient in the way it manages its inventories and trade receivables; problems in this area may be identified by the working capital efficiency ratios described above. It may also be that the company has accumulated a large cash balance for which it is unable to find an immediate investment opportunity; this may provoke concerns that the management are unable to develop an effective growth strategy, or generate ideas for product innovation.

Financing structure and risk ratios

Financial structure and risk ratios are used to measure financial strength.

The table below shows the two ratios that deal with the firm's solvency – its ability to meet its long-term liabilities.

ASSOCIATED BRITISH FOODS PLC	RATIO ANALYSIS				
	2015	2014	2013	2012	2011
Capital structure ratios					
Debt (financial gearing) ratio	11.4%	11.8%	14.2%	17.7%	19.4%
Interest cover	15.5	14.8	10.9	7.7	8.3

Gearing ratio or debt ratio

The gearing ratio, or debt ratio, is used to assess the company's ability to meet its long-term liabilities. The gearing ratio (leverage ratio in the US) is a measure of how much of the company's capital employed is provided by debt, defined as 'total negotiated interest bearing borrowings'.

$$Gearing\ ratio\ =\ \frac{Total\ interest\ bearing\ borrowings}{Capital\ employed}\ \times\ 100$$

Loan interest and capital repayments have to be made regardless of the firm's profit and cash flow in the period, so the level of debt in a business is also a measure of the risk to which a prospective lender or investor is exposed.

Interest cover

The interest cover ratio is a measure of how easy it is for the company to cover the interest payable on borrowings from its operating profit.

$$Interest\ cover\ =\ \frac{Operating\ profit}{Interest\ payable}$$

Shareholder return ratios

These measures assess the returns to the firm's shareholders, reflecting the relationship between share price, dividends and profit.

The table below shows three of the financial ratios that look at the company's financial performance from the perspective of the firm's shareholders.

ASSOCIATED BRITISH FOODS PLC	RATIO ANALYSIS				
	2015	**2014**	**2013**	**2012**	**2011**
Shareholder return ratios					
Return on equity	8.4%	11.8%	9.6%	9.5%	9.4%
Price/earnings ratio	45.4	26.6	23.4	17.4	15.1
Dividend yield	1.1%	1.3%	1.8%	2.3%	2.4%

Return on equity (ROE)

ROE measures the after-tax profit available for the company's shareholders as a percentage of shareholders' equity.

$$Return\ on\ equity\ = \frac{Profit\ after\ tax\ attributable\ to\ shareholders}{Shareholders'equity} \times 100$$

ROE is a useful, but simple, measure of profitability. ROE is affected by the rate at which net profit is produced from sales revenue and by asset use efficiency, in a similar way to which profit margin and net asset turnover affect the RONA measure described above. But ROE is also affected by the proportion of debt capital and equity capital employed in the business. The section below describes the way in which this affects ROE and how DuPont analysis can highlight how ROE is influenced by these various factors.

Three-Step DuPont analysis

The relationship between the three factors that affect the level of ROE was first identified by the DuPont company in the 1920s. Their ROE analysis was extended to highlight the underlying drivers of profitability. The resulting Three-Step DuPont analysis separates ROE into three key components:

1. Operating efficiency: measured by profit margin.

2. Asset use efficiency: measured by total asset turnover.

3. Gearing: measured by the gearing factor.

The table below shows these three DuPont ratios for ABF:

ASSOCIATED BRITISH FOODS PLC	RATIO ANALYSIS				
	2015	2014	2013	2012	2011
DuPont analysis					
Profit margin	4.2%	5.9%	4.4%	4.5%	4.9%
Total asset turnover	1.2	1.2	1.3	1.2	1.1
Gearing factor	1.6	1.6	1.7	1.8	1.8

The relationship between these three components is reflected in the formula:

$$ROE \ = \ Profit\ margin \ \times \ asset\ turnover \ \times \ gearing\ factor$$

Using Three-Step DuPont analysis

The three components of the DuPont analysis are calculated as:

$$Profit\ margin \ = \ \frac{Profit\ after\ tax\ attributable\ to\ shareholders}{Shareholders'equity} \ \times\ 100$$

$$Total\ asset\ turnover \ = \ \frac{Sales\ revenue}{Total\ assets}$$

$$Gearing\ factor \ = \ \frac{Total\ assets}{Shareholders'equity}$$

The example below illustrates how higher financial gearing can flatter the ROE performance of a company with lower profit margin and asset efficiency.

Balance sheet – £000's	ABC Limited	XYZ Limited
Total assets	25,000	25,000
Shareholders' equity	5,000	10,000

Profit statement – £000's		
Sales	10,000	15,000
Net profit	2,000	4,000
Return on equity	40%	40%

Applying the Three-Step DuPont analysis reveals the following:

	ABC Limited	XYZ Limited
Profit margin	20%	27%
Asset turnover	0.4	0.6
Gearing factor	5.0	2.5
Return on Equity	40%	40%

The DuPont analysis reveals that, although both companies appear to deliver the same value for shareholders, measured by ROE, there are quite significant differences in the means by which this is achieved. ABC does not perform as well as XYZ in terms of profit and asset efficiency, but its high gearing improves ROE. In other words, although the financial return on the assets is lower for ABC, a significantly lower proportion of the firm's assets are funded by its shareholders and their share of the profit that is left after paying debt interest and tax represents a greater percentage of the shareholder funds than is the case in XYZ.

Earnings per share (EPS)

EPS is a measure of the profit after taxation (and preference share dividend, if any) per equity share in issue during the course of a financial year. If new shares have been issued during the year, a weighted average is used for EPS.

Price/earnings ratio (P/E ratio)

Market price is influenced by, amongst other factors, the expected future profits of the business. The price/earnings ratio reflects the market's view of the quality and sustainability of the company's profits, as well as the potential for future profit growth. The higher the ratio, the greater the value the market places on the company in terms of its potential to generate future profits.

$$Price/earnings\ ratio\ = \frac{Market\ price\ per\ share}{Earnings\ per\ share}$$

Dividend yield

Dividend yield is an important measure for shareholders who are looking for income from shares rather than focusing on share price growth potential.

$$Dividend \; yield = \frac{Dividend \; per \; share}{Market \; price \; per \; share} \times 100$$

Cash flow ratios

The cash flow statement sets out information that helps to evaluate changes in the company's net assets and in its financial structure. Cash flow ratios provide further insights into the liquidity and solvency of the company and help to assess the firm's ability to generate cash. Unlike measures based on profits, cash flow ratios cannot be affected by the different accounting policies used by different companies.

The table below shows the four cash flow ratios that are helpful in assessing the company's capacity to generate cash from its sales revenues and the extent to which these cash flows meet the firm's liabilities.

ASSOCIATED BRITISH FOODS PLC	RATIO ANALYSIS				
	2015	2014	2013	2012	2011
Cash flow ratios					
Operating cash flow ratio	0.4	0.5	0.5	0.5	0.3
Price/cash flow ratio	20.7	14.1	10.8	7.8	11.1
Cash flow margin ratio	9.1%	11.1%	9.6%	10.1%	6.7%
Cash flow to debt ratio	35.1%	43.7%	38.7%	35.4%	21.4%

Operating cash flow ratio

Cash flow is an indication of how cash moves into and out of the company and how the firm is able to meet its liabilities. In other words, it is a measure of short-term liquidity. The operating cash flow ratio compares the cash flow generated from the company's operations during the year against its current liabilities at the end of the year. It provides an indication of how easily the business can meet its short-term liabilities from the cash it has generated from its operations during the year.

$$Operating\ cash\ flow\ ratio\ =\ \frac{Cash\ flow\ from\ operations}{Current\ liabilities}$$

Price/cash flow ratio

This ratio can sometimes be a better indication of a company's value than the more frequently used price/earnings ratio. It compares the company's share price to the cash flow the company generates on a per share basis.

$$Price/cash\ flow\ ratio\ =\ \frac{Market\ price\ per\ share}{Operating\ cash\ flow\ per\ share}$$

Cash flow margin ratio

The cash flow margin ratio measures the cash the company generates from its operations against its sales revenue. A high ratio indicates that a company is efficient at converting its sales to cash.

$$Cash\ flow\ margin\ ratio\ =\ \frac{Cash\ flow\ from\ operations}{Sales\ revenue}\ \times\ 100$$

Cash flow to debt ratio

The cash flow to debt ratio compares the company's operating cash flows to its total debt, which includes trade credit, the current portion of long-term debt and long-term debt. The ratio provides an indication of a company's ability to cover total debt from its annual operating cash flow.

$$Cash\ flow\ to\ debt\ ratio\ =\ \frac{Cash\ flow\ from\ operations}{Total\ debt}\ \times\ 100$$

Comparing financial indicators for different companies

It can be helpful to compare the financial indicators for different companies. Investors may find it useful as a means of identifying the companies that are the best managed and deliver better results. Managers may also find it useful to compare their results to a competitor to benchmark the performance of their own company and identify possible areas for improvement.

But it is important to be aware of the constraints on making direct comparisons and the adjustments that may be necessary to make a fair comparison. For example:

- Many large international companies are collections of several types of businesses in more than one country; this can affect revenue generation, cost structure, and asset and working capital requirements. Financial reports may not provide sufficient information to make a detailed segmental analysis on which to base comparable financial indicators.

- Depending on the location of their parent company, large international firms may be using either US accounting rules, European (IFRS) accounting rules, or the rules of their home country. This may result in significant differences in the way that some material items are treated. For example, financial instruments and leasing contracts.

- There can be material differences in the way that the company's own accounting policies affect items like depreciation and inventory valuation.

- Net asset values can be significantly affected by the way in which brands and other intangible assets are treated. Purchased intangibles are shown on the balance sheet at adjusted cost, whilst intangibles built up in the business will not have any value in the balance sheet.

Chapter 4

Model 2A: Sales Forecasting

Financial models are often used to make forecasts of sales volumes and revenues in order to help businesses in their decision-making. An analysis of past data may be a suitable starting point for a sales forecast when trends and other variations are clear, relatively stable, and when future conditions are expected to be broadly the same as the periods from which the past data was collected. When several years' data becomes available, time series analysis can be used to identify different types of variations.

Identifying trends and other variations in time series data

A data time series records a series of values over a period of time; analysis of this time series data may identify:

- **Cyclical variations**: Medium-term changes that repeat in cycles which may be caused by factors arising from trade and economic events.

- **Seasonal variations**: Short-term fluctuations due to factors that affect results at different times of the year.

- **Random variations**: Changes in recorded data due to multiple factors not related to seasonal or cyclical patterns, or long-term trends.

- **Trends**: An upward or downward pattern that can be observed over a number of periods. If future conditions are expected to be similar to those in the past, this trend may be extended and used as the basis for a forecast.

The following variations can be seen in the sales volume chart in Figure 4.1:

- The cyclical effect of the global financial crisis on sales, from 2008 to 2009.

- Seasonal variations in sales that repeat over the whole time series.

- A sustained upward trend in sales from 2010 onwards.

Figure 4.1: Quarterly sales 2005–2015 – 000's units

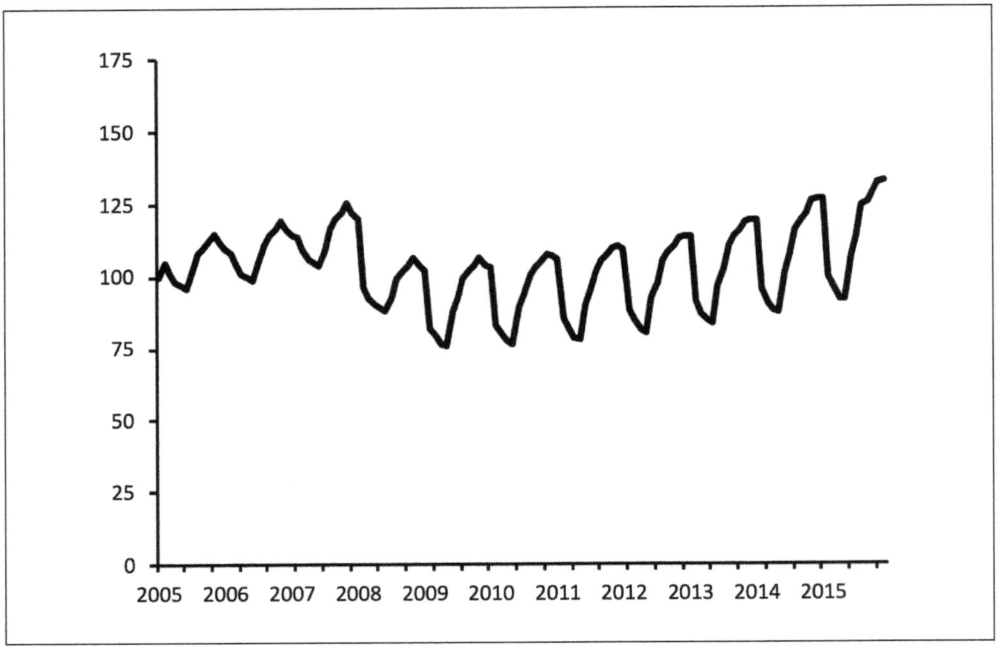

Using an Excel chart to identify a trend

The time series data below show a company's quarterly sales volumes for 20 consecutive quarters.

Quarterly sales – ooo's				
	1	2	3	4
2010	362	264	482	635
2011	432	322	552	715
2012	493	373	628	793
2013	560	433	708	887
2014	623	479	779	980

There appears to be some seasonal variation to the data and underlying growth over this five-year period. These patterns become much clearer when the data is charted in Excel:

- Select the Insert option from the menu at the top of the screen.

- Click on the line chart option from the Chart section.

Screenshot 4.1

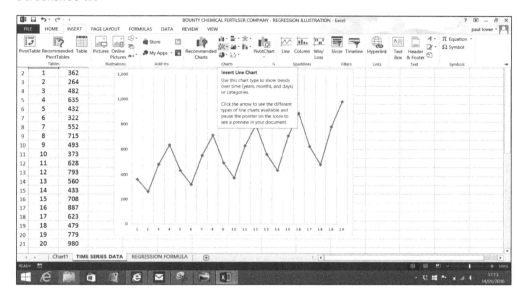

Screenshot 4.1 reveals clear repetitive variations in the level of quarterly sales, as well as showing an upward trend. Excel can add a trend line to the graph as a 'line of best fit' through the data. Follow these steps to add a trend line to the chart:

- Click anywhere in the chart. This displays the Excel chart tools.

- Click on the Design tab to display the Add Chart Element tab.

- Click on the Add Chart Element dropdown list to display options.

- Select Trendline to display trend line charting options.

- Select the Linear option from the dropdown list.

Screenshot 4.2

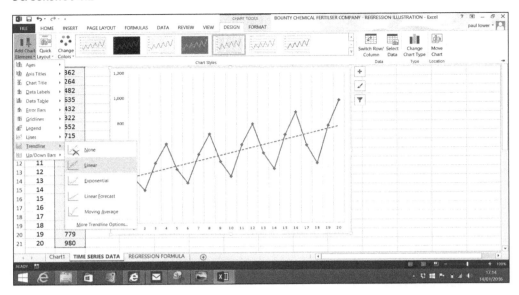

Excel uses a statistical method known as linear regression to calculate the values with which to draw the trend line; the function for the straight line takes the form:

$$y = bx + a$$

The value for coefficient b represents the slope on the line; in other words, the rate at which the trend increases in each quarter. The coefficient a represents the point at which the trend line intersects the vertical axis. When values for a and b are known, a value for y can be calculated for any value of x. One way to find the values for the a and b coefficients is to display the function for the trend line on the chart:

- Click on the Trendline on the chart to select it.

- Right click and select Format Trendline.

- Select Trendline Options from the menu.

- Select Display Equation on chart from the menu.

Screenshot 4.3

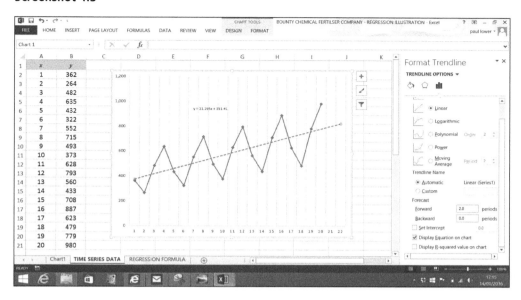

Excel displays the function for the trend line as: $y = 21.295x + 351.41$

The Sales Forecasting Model

- **Users:** This financial model would typically be used by a financial analyst or a financial planning manager to make a sales forecast when future conditions are expected to be broadly the same as in the recent past.

- **Purpose:** To use time series data to identify and isolate trends and other variations in past sales data, to use as the basis for a forecast.

- **Outputs:** A projected trend for the forecast period, adjusted by a seasonal index to produce a sales forecast.

- **Calculations:** Isolation of trend values for each period of time series data, using Excel functions SLOPE and INTERCEPT. Seasonal and random variations in the time series data are derived from actual data and trend values, and are used to compile a seasonal index base.

- **Inputs:** Monthly or quarterly sales data.

- **Design:** Sales data is entered onto the INPUT sheet. The three calculation and output sheets are comprised of:

  - ANALYSIS

  - SEASONAL INDEX

- FORECAST

Refer to the Excel workbook: SALES FORECAST MODEL.xlsx

Using Excel functions to isolate a trend from time series data

The worksheet named 'ANALYSIS' takes the sales data from the 'INPUT' worksheet. In column B the quarterly values are numbered from 1 to 20, representing the x values. The Excel SLOPE function returns the slope of the trend line; in other words, the b coefficient for the straight-line function $y = bx + a$. The correct syntax for the function is: SLOPE (known_y's,known_x's):

Screenshot 4.4

E3			fx	=SLOPE(C6:C25,B6:B25)			
	A	B	C	D	E	F	G
1	**TIME SERIES ANALYSIS**						
2							
3				b coefficient =	21.295	a coefficient =	351.4
4	Quarter		Sales	Trend	Variation		
5		x	000's	$y = bx+a$	Sales/Trend		
6	2010 - 1	1	362	373	0.97		
7	2	2	264	394	0.67		
8	3	3	482	415	1.16		
9	4	4	635	437	1.45		
10	2011 - 1	5	432	458	0.94		
11	2	6	322	479	0.67		

The SLOPE function in cell E3 gives a value of 21.295 for the b coefficient.

The Excel INTERCEPT function calculates the point at which a line will intersect the vertical y-axis; in other words, the a coefficient for the straight-line function. The correct syntax for the function is: INTERCEPT (known_y's,known_x's):

Screenshot 4.5

	G3				✗ ✓	fx	=INTERCEPT(C6:C25,B6:B25)	
	A	B	C	D	E	F	G	
1	TIME SERIES ANALYSIS							
2								
3					*b* coefficient =	21.295	*a* coefficient =	351.4
4	Quarter			Sales	Trend	Variation		
5		*x*		000's	*y = bx+a*	Sales/Trend		
6	2010 - 1	1		362	373	0.97		
7	2	2		264	394	0.67		
8	3	3		482	415	1.16		
9	4	4		635	437	1.45		
10	2011 - 1	5		432	458	0.94		
11	2	6		322	479	0.67		

The INTERCEPT function in cell G3 produces a value of 351.4 for the *a* coefficient. The value of *y* can now be calculated for any value of *x* using the straight line function and the values for the *a* and *b* coefficients. This produces the trend values for column D:

Screenshot 4.6

	D6				✗ ✓	fx	=E$3*B6+G$3	
	A	B	C	D	E	F	G	
1	TIME SERIES ANALYSIS							
2								
3					*b* coefficient =	21.295	*a* coefficient =	351.4
4	Quarter			Sales	Trend	Variation		
5		*x*		000's	*y = bx+a*	Sales/Trend		
6	2010 - 1	1		362	373	0.97		
7	2	2		264	394	0.67		
8	3	3		482	415	1.16		
9	4	4		635	437	1.45		
10	2011 - 1	5		432	458	0.94		
11	2	6		322	479	0.67		

Calculating seasonal and random variations

The data shows both an upward trend and repeated variations of this trend, which may be comprised of seasonal and random variations. These can now be quantified by dividing the sales value by the trend value:

Screenshot 4.7

E6			▾	⋮	✕	✓	fx	=C6/D6		
	A	B	C		D	E		F		G
1	TIME SERIES ANALYSIS									
2										
3					b coefficient =	21.295		a coefficient =		351.4
4	Quarter		Sales		Trend	Variation				
5		x	000's		$y = bx+a$	Sales/Trend				
6	2010 - 1	1	362		373	0.97				
7	2	2	264		394	0.67				
8	3	3	482		415	1.16				
9	4	4	635		437	1.45				
10	2011 - 1	5	432		458	0.94				
11	2	6	322		479	0.67				

Calculating a seasonal index

An average is calculated for the quarterly variations and this will provide a seasonal index to be used for the sales forecast:

Screenshot 4.8

B3					fx	=ANALYSIS!E6		
	A	B	C	D	E	F	G	
1	**SEASONAL INDEX**							
2	QUARTER	1	2	3	4			
3	2010	0.97	0.67	1.16	1.45			
4	2011	0.94	0.67	1.10	1.37			
5	2012	0.91	0.66	1.07	1.31			
6	2013	0.89	0.67	1.06	1.28			
7	2014	0.87	0.65	1.03	1.26			
8	**AVERAGE**	0.92	0.66	1.08	1.33			

Extending the trend for the sales forecast

If the economic and market conditions during the forecast period are expected to be broadly the same as in the past, it might reasonably be assumed that the trend will continue to rise in the same way. To extend the trend for eight quarters, the values in column C can be calculated using new *x* values, ranging from 21 to 28:

Screenshot 4.9

C4					fx	=B4*ANALYSIS!E$3+ANALYSIS!G$3		
	A	B	C	D	E	F	G	
1	**SALES FORECAST**							
2	Quarter		Trend	Seasonal	Forecast			
3		*x*	*y = bx+a*	index	000's			
4	2015 - 1	21	799	0.92	733			
5	2	22	820	0.66	545			
6	3	23	841	1.08	912			
7	4	24	862	1.33	1151			
8	2016 - 1	25	884	0.92	811			
9	2	26	905	0.66	601			
10	3	27	926	1.08	1005			
11	4	28	948	1.33	1265			

Adjusting the trend for seasonal variations

Each value in the time series data for the period 2010 to 2014 includes a trend component and seasonal and random variation components. By their very nature, random variations cannot be predicted, so for the purposes of the sales forecast they are assumed to be zero. By applying the seasonal index to the extended trend value, an adjustment can be made to add seasonal variations to the sales forecast:

Screenshot 4.10

E4					f_x	=C4*D4		
	A	B	C	D	E	F	G
1	SALES FORECAST						
2	Quarter		Trend	Seasonal	Forecast		
3		x	$y = bx+a$	index	000's		
4	2015 - 1	21	799	0.92	733		
5	2	22	820	0.66	545		
6	3	23	841	1.08	912		
7	4	24	862	1.33	1151		
8	2016 - 1	25	884	0.92	811		
9	2	26	905	0.66	601		
10	3	27	926	1.08	1005		
11	4	28	948	1.33	1265		

When good quality data is available for time series analysis, and when economic and market conditions in the future are expected to be broadly the same as they were during the period from which the data has been collected, this kind of financial model can be a useful tool to help in forecasting sales. A similar approach to making a forecast of business costs is described in the next chapter.

Chapter 5

Model 2B:
Cost Forecasting

I n the previous chapter, reference was made to the linear regression function being
used to isolate trends and in time series data as the basis for sales forecasts. A similar
approach can be used to build a financial model to forecast business costs.

Causal analysis

Causal analysis attempts to establish and test the relationship between the independent
variables to be forecast and the other variables that are dependent on them. For example,
machine operating hours (an independent variable) and machine maintenance costs
(a dependent variable). Screenshot 5.1 shows production operating hours and machine
maintenance costs for 36 consecutive months.

Screenshot 5.1

Operating Hours	Maintenance Cost	Operating Hours	Maintenance Cost
2782	23618	2449	24482
2531	22521	1853	17189
2788	21000	2500	23007
3033	24306	3109	22814
1612	18448	1619	20500
3381	28083	1634	17522
2354	19988	1908	18913
1718	17567	2498	23271
2085	19325	1432	15699
2908	27983	1434	15699
1021	15114	1216	13995
2419	19150	2956	25440
2775	24551	2830	25444
1574	16300	2984	23230
2159	21885	2102	19857
3305	29732	2963	27655
2037	21150	2665	22226
2418	20450	1857	21127

It is clear from the Screenshot 5.1 data that, as one might expect, there is a relationship between machine usage and the level of machine maintenance costs. If a company operates a preventative maintenance programme and carries out periodic servicing, it is likely that fixed machine maintenance costs will be incurred regardless of the operating hours. But other maintenance costs, such as machine tool replacement and lubricants, will tend to increase as machine usage increases. When the machine hours and maintenance costs are plotted on a scatter diagram in Excel, this relationship is clear:

- Select the relevant data in columns B and C.

- Select the Insert option from the menu at the top of the screen.

- Click on the Scatter Diagram option from the Chart section.

- Click on the first option on the top left.

Screenshot 5.2

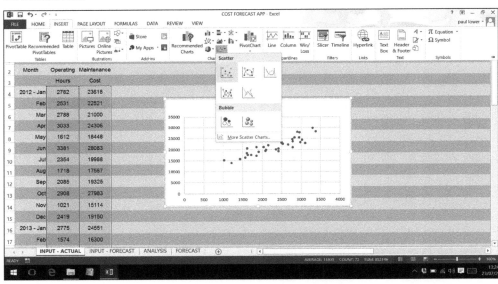

Adding a line of best fit through the data

Excel can add a line of best fit through the plotted data by following these steps:

- Click anywhere in the chart; this will display the Excel chart tools.

- Click on the Design tab to display the Add Chart Element tab.

- Click on the Add Chart Element dropdown list to display options.

- Select Trendline to display trend line charting options.

- Select the Linear option from the dropdown list.

Screenshot 5.3

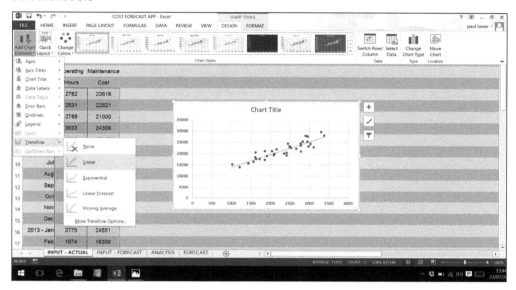

The scatter diagram reveals a strong linear relationship between operating hours and maintenance costs. The data plots are grouped quite tightly around the line of best fit.

Using correlation to test the strength of the relationship

Correlation is a statistical tool that describes the extent to which two variables are related, illustrated by the three scatter diagrams in Figure 5.1.

Figure 5.1: Scatter diagrams

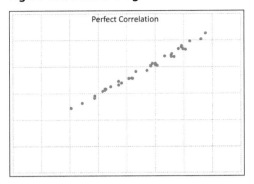

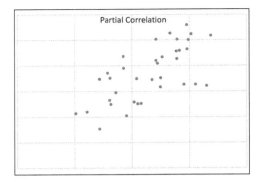

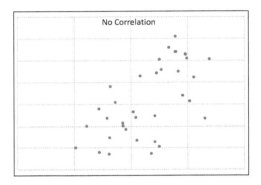

Correlation measures how close the points on a scatter diagram lie to a straight line. It is rare to find perfect correlation in real-life examples. As in the machine example above, it is more usual to find some degree of partial correlation, or no correlation at all. When low values of one variable are associated with low values of another, or when high values of one are associated with high values of another, the two variables are positively correlated. Variables are negatively correlated when low values of one variable are associated with the high values of the other, and vice versa.

Measuring correlation

Correlation is measured using the Pearsonian coefficient of correlation, which calculates a value for r between +1 and -1. If the plotted points lie exactly on a straight line with a positive slope, r will be equal to 1. If the data points lie along a straight line with a negative slope, r will be equal to -1. The further the points are scattered around the line, the closer the value of r will become to zero. When r is equal to 0 there is no linear relationship between the two sets of variables.

Using the Excel CORREL function

The CORREL function returns the correlation coefficient of two arrays of data. The correct syntax for the function is: CORREL(array1, array2).

The Cost Forecasting Model

- **Users:** This financial model would normally be used by a financial analyst or financial planning manager to make a cost forecast when a strong linear relationship exists between an independent variable, like machine operating hours, and a dependent variable, such as maintenance costs.

- **Purpose:** To use Excel linear regression and correlation functions to measure and quantify the causal link between independent and dependent variables, and use this relationship as the basis of a cost forecast.

- **Outputs:** A cost forecast for the dependent variable.

- **Calculations:** Excel functions SLOPE and INTERCEPT are used to identify the fixed and variable components of machine maintenance costs. The Excel CORREL function is used to test the strength of the relationship between the independent and dependent variables. These are then used to forecast machine maintenance costs for various operating hours.

- **Inputs:** Known values for the independent and dependent variables.

- **Design:** Known data for monthly operating hours and maintenance costs are entered into the INPUT – ACTUAL sheet. Forecast machine operating hours are entered to the INPUT – FORECAST sheet. Two calculation and output sheets comprise:

  - ANALYSIS

  - FORECAST

Refer to the Excel workbook: COST FORECAST MODEL.xlsx

Using Excel functions to identify variable and fixed costs

The ANALYSIS worksheet takes the operating hours data from the INPUT – ACTUAL sheet for the independent variable x in column B. The data for the dependent variable y is taken from the same input sheet. The Excel function SLOPE is used to calculate the b coefficient for the straight line function $y = bx + a$. The correct syntax for the function is: SLOPE (known_y's,known_x's).

Screenshot 5.4

B2		▾	:	✕	✓	*fx*	=SLOPE(C6:C41,B6:B41)

	A	B	C	D	E	F	G
1	**DATA ANALYSIS**						
2	*b* coefficient =	5.68	*a* coefficient = 8294		Correlation *r* = 0.9036		
3		Operating	Maintenance				
4	Month	Hours	Costs				
5		*x*	*y*				
6	2012 - Jan	2782	23618				
7	Feb	2531	22521				
8	Mar	2788	21000				
9	Apr	3033	24306				
10	May	1612	18448				
11	Jun	3381	28083				

The SLOPE function in cell B2 gives a value of £5.68 for the *b* coefficient. This represents the rate at which the maintenance costs increase in relation to an increase in operating hours. In other words, the variable cost component.

The Excel INTERCEPT function calculates the point at which a line will intersect the vertical y-axis; in other words, the *a* coefficient for the straight-line function. The correct syntax for the function is: INTERCEPT (known_y's,known_x's).

Screenshot 5.5

D2		▾	:	✕	✓	*fx*	=INTERCEPT(C6:C41,B6:B41)

	A	B	C	D	E	F	G
1	**DATA ANALYSIS**						
2	*b* coefficient =	5.68	*a* coefficient =	8294	Correlation *r* = 0.9036		
3		Operating	Maintenance				
4	Month	Hours	Costs				
5		*x*	*y*				
6	2012 - Jan	2782	23618				
7	Feb	2531	22521				
8	Mar	2788	21000				
9	Apr	3033	24306				
10	May	1612	18448				
11	Jun	3381	28083				

The INTERCEPT function in cell D2 produces a value of £8,294 for the *a* coefficient, which represents the fixed element of the maintenance costs. The value of *y* can now be calculated for any value of *x* using the straight-line function $y = bx + a$. The values for the *a* and *b* coefficients are calculated by Excel.

Screenshot 5.6

	A	B	C	D	E	F	G
F2				f_x	=CORREL(C6:C41,B6:B41)		
1	**DATA ANALYSIS**						
2	*b* coefficient= 5.68		*a* coefficient= 8294		Correlation *r* =	0.9036	
3		Operating	Maintenance				
4	Month	Hours	Costs				
5		*x*	*y*				
6	2012 - Jan	2782	23618				
7	Feb	2531	22521				
8	Mar	2788	21000				
9	Apr	3033	24306				
10	May	1612	18448				
11	Jun	3381	28083				

Correlation and causation

The Excel CORREL function has produced a value in cell F2 of $r = 0.9036$, indicating a high degree of positive correlation between the machine operating hours and the maintenance costs. A second test, referred to as R-squared, or the coefficient of determination, is also used to test the extent to which changes in the value of 'y' can be explained by changes in the value of 'x'. As the name suggests, the coefficient of determination is calculated by multiplying the Pearsonian coefficient 'r' by itself.

As a general rule, when R-squared is equal to at least 0.8, the link between *x* and *y* is assumed to be a strong link between these two sets of variables. Some degree of caution is needed though. High values for the correlation and the coefficient of determination do not necessarily prove causation; this may have been caused purely by chance. But the greater number of pairs of variables there are in a data sample, the less likely it is that the correlation is coincidental. In this particular example, there is a logical relationship between the operating hours and the maintenance costs – and a high correlation confirms this causative link.

Making a maintenance cost forecast

The forecast of operating hours for the next 12 months is entered onto the worksheet INPUT – FORECAST.

Screenshot 5.7

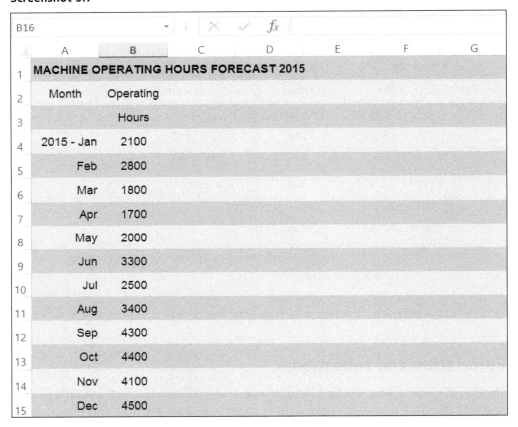

B16					f_x		
	A	B	C	D	E	F	G
1	MACHINE OPERATING HOURS FORECAST 2015						
2	Month	Operating					
3		Hours					
4	2015 - Jan	2100					
5	Feb	2800					
6	Mar	1800					
7	Apr	1700					
8	May	2000					
9	Jun	3300					
10	Jul	2500					
11	Aug	3400					
12	Sep	4300					
13	Oct	4400					
14	Nov	4100					
15	Dec	4500					

These values are used by the FORECAST worksheet for the x values in column B, representing the independent variable.

Screenshot 5.8

B6			▼	⋮	✕	✓	*fx*	='INPUT - FORECAST'!B4		

	A	B	C	D	E	F	G
1	**MAINTENANCE COST FORECAST 2015**						
2							
3		Operating	Maintenance				
4	Month	Hours	Costs				
5		x	$y = bx+a$				
6	2015 - Jan	2100	20215				
7	Feb	2800	24189				
8	Mar	1800	18512				
9	Apr	1700	17944				
10	May	2000	19647				
11	Jun	3300	27027				
12	Jul	2500	22486				
13	Aug	3400	27595				
14	Sep	4300	32704				
15	Oct	4400	33272				
16	Nov	4100	31569				
17	Dec	4500	33840				

The value of y, the machine maintenance costs, can now be calculated for any value of x using the straight-line function. The values for the a and b coefficients are picked up from the ANALYSIS worksheet.

Screenshot 5.9

	A	B	C	D	E	F	G
C6			fx	=ANALYSIS!B$2*FORECAST!B6+ANALYSIS!D$2			
1	MAINTENANCE COST FORECAST 2015						
2							
3		Operating	Maintenance				
4	Month	Hours	Costs				
5		x	$y = bx+a$				
6	2015 - Jan	2100	20215				
7	Feb	2800	24189				
8	Mar	1800	18512				
9	Apr	1700	17944				
10	May	2000	19647				
11	Jun	3300	27027				

The y values in column C of the FORECAST worksheet represent the corresponding value on the line of best fit for each of the x values. When there is high correlation between the two variables, the data points will lie close to the line and the forecast value for the dependent value may be expected to be reasonably accurate. A lower correlation will result when the data points are more scattered around the line of best fit, and a wider margin of forecast error may be expected.

Interpolation and extrapolation

The input data for the machine operating hours, the independent variable x, is in the range 1,021 to 3,381 hours and the linear relationship between the machine usage and the maintenance costs is based on this recorded data.

Figure 5.2: Resin processing machines – monthly maintenance costs

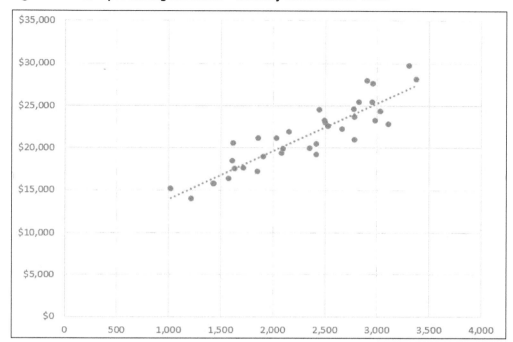

The forecast values for *x* in the period January to July 2015 fall within the same range as the recorded actual data. Using an approach referred to as interpolation, the relationship between *x* and *y* is assumed to be the same because the forecast values fall within the range of observed data values.

The forecast values for *x* in the period August to December 2015 fall outside the range of recorded data. Using an approach referred to as extrapolation, it has been assumed that the linear relationship between *x* and *y* will remain the same; the relationship is within the observed data values. But this may not be the case. At much higher levels of machine usage it is possible that greater wear and tear will result in expendable parts and lubricants being used at a higher rate. For this reason care needs to be taken when relying on extrapolation of causal relationships for forecasting.

Effective product pricing and profit improvement strategies are both based on a sound understanding of business cost behaviour. Chapter 7 looks at this in more detail, and describes how a financial model can be used to assist.

Chapter 6

Model 3: Cash Flow Forecasting

The increase or decrease in the level of cash and other highly liquid financial assets held by a business from one period to the next is referred to as positive or negative cash flow. But the term cash flow also describes the process in which cash flows into, circulates inside, and flows out of a business.

Cash flow is the lifeblood of any enterprise. In the same way that blood carries oxygen around the human body to provide energy and vitality, so cash flow is at the heart of a healthy business.

At an operational level, the importance of cash has long been recognised as the essential means of exchange by which new resource inputs, in the form of materials and labour, are acquired, and the way in which the value of the firm's output is monetised. In other words, cash provides the means by which the firm flourishes and grows. For those managers and businesses that are unable to understand the vital importance of cash flow, the price of failure is very high. A study of bankruptcy statistics for small and medium-sized enterprises shows that cash flow failure is the root cause of many of them, even though a significant proportion of those insolvent companies were actually profitable at the time of their demise.

Cash flow is also a key driver of shareholder value. Profit was traditionally recognised as the yardstick by which shareholder value was measured. Established business valuation methods viewed the worth of a company in relation to, and as a multiple of, its profits. But the modern approach views shareholder value as the function of a firm's ability to generate future free cash flows (FCF); in other words, the unencumbered cash a company generates after meeting its essential operating costs and investing to maintain its productive assets. FCF is a measure of how much cash a business has available to service debt or pay dividends. The Shareholder Value Added approach to business valuation (discussed in Chapter 10) bases enterprise value on the present value of the company's future free cash flows. So it is now widely recognised that strong cash flow is not only the lifeblood of a healthy business operation, it is also one of the best indicators of the real value of a company.

For this reason, cash flow forecasting is one of the key tools in planning for the continued survival and success of any business – using assumptions about the timing and size of cash flows to highlight funds available for investment, or identifying additional finance requirements and allowing sufficient time to negotiate and secure appropriate funding facilities.

The Cash Flow Forecasting Model

- **Users:** A financial analyst, or financial planning manager would typically use this financial model to make a cash flow forecast.

- **Purpose:** To use a set of key cash flow driver assumptions to produce a cash flow forecast that can be used to test the sensitivity of the forecast against various types of risk. The illustrative Excel workbook is set up as a monthly forecast, but the same principles apply for an annual or quarterly forecast. It is only necessary to change the labels for each column of the forecast.

- **Outputs:** A cash flow forecast using the format of a cash flow statement.

- **Inputs:** Most of the input assumptions for the cash flow forecast are expressed as cash flows in thousands. The cost of goods sold is input as a percentage of the sales revenue forecast. The inputs for the working capital components are based on the working capital efficiency metrics in Chapter 3. For example, Days' Sales Outstanding (DSO) and Days' Sales in Inventory (DSI).

- **Calculations:** Most elements of the cash flow forecast are picked up directly from the input sheet. The cost of goods sold is calculated as a percentage of sales revenue. The inputs for the working capital components allow the models to establish a dynamic link between changes in the level of sales activity and the inventory and trade credit needed to support it.

- **Design:** Assumptions are entered into the INPUT sheet. Calculation and output is in the CASH FLOW FORECAST sheet. Refer to the Excel workbook: CASH FLOW FORECAST MODEL.xlsx

Topic refresher – understanding business cash flow

Business cash flow is a function of the cash generated by, or used in:

- Operating activities.

- Investing activities: The purchases of, or the sale of, property, plant and equipment.

- Financing activities: New share capital issues or loans, repayment of loans or dividend payments.

Calculating cash flow for a period

Cash flow for a period is equal to the change in the cash held at the end of the period compared to the cash at the start of the period. It can be calculated as:

- Cash generated from or used in **operating** activities: A.

- Cash received from or used in **investing** activities: B.

- Cash received from or used in **financing** activities: C.

- Cash flow: Increase or decrease in cash in the period A+B+C.

Cash generated from operating activities (operating cash flow)

Operating profit is not the same thing as operating cash flow; profit is calculated on an accruals basis, which means that:

- Sales revenue is included in the profit calculation to the extent that it has been invoiced to customers, even though it may take 30 days or more before the company receives payment in cash from its customers.

- Costs are included to the extent that they have been incurred, and match the sales revenue generated in the same period, even though the suppliers of the goods and services concerned may not expect to receive payment in cash for a month or so.

- The cost of inventory is included to the extent that it has been sold in the period, or used to make something that has been sold in the period.

- The cash cost of purchases of property, plant and equipment is not included, but a depreciation charge is made in each period to reflect the reduction in the value of these assets as they are being used. Depreciation is deducted in calculating profit but does not represent an actual movement of cash. Other similar non-cash items include amortisation charges relating to intangible assets and any impairment charges made in respect of adjustments to the fair value of any assets.

These factors explain why there is a difference between operating profit and operating cash flow in any particular period. But, as timing differences unwind, customers settle their invoices and suppliers are paid. The company will, of course, see the profit excluding non-cash charges converted into additional cash funds and this must be reflected in any calculation of business cash flow.

There are two approaches to calculate the cash generated by or used in the company's operating activities: the direct method and indirect method. These two approaches are illustrated based on the income statement and balance sheet for the Omega Trading Company below.

OMEGA TRADING COMPANY LIMITED

Income statement for year ending 31st December

$000's omitted	2015	2014
Sales	120,000	118,000
Cost of goods sold	(77,160)	(73,160)
Gross profit	42,840	44,840
Administrative expenses	(18,500)	(17,100)
Operating profit	**13,340**	**17,240**
Finance costs	(750)	(750)
Profit before tax	12,590	16,490
Taxation	(3,148)	(4,123)
PROFIT AFTER TAX	**9,442**	**12,367**

OMEGA TRADING COMPANY LIMITED

Balance sheet as at 31st December

$000's omitted	2015	2014
Non-current assets		
Property, plant and equipment	36,300	34,800
	36,300	34,800
Current assets		
Stock	41,795	36,580
Trade debtors	24,658	22,630
Cash and cash equivalents	5,783	4,332
	72,236	63,542

Current liabilities

Trade and other creditors	(6,765)	(6,013)
	(6,765)	(6,013)
Net current assets	65,471	57,529

Non-current liabilities

Borrowings	(15,000)	(15,000)
NET ASSETS	**86,771**	**77,329**
Share capital	30,000	30,000
Retained earnings	56,771	47,329
SHAREHOLDERS' EQUITY	**86,771**	**77,329**

Direct method of calculating operating cash flow

OMEGA TRADING COMPANY LIMITED

Direct method of calculating cash generated from activities

$000's omitted	2015
Cash receipts from customers	117,973
Cash payments to suppliers	(81,623)
Cash payments to employees	(11,000)
Cash paid for other operating expenses	(14,500)
Cash generated from operations	**10,849**
Interest charges paid	(750)
Tax paid	(3,148)
Net cash generated from operating activities	**6,951**

Purchase of plant and equipment	(5,500)
Net cash used in investing activities	**(5,500)**
Repayment of borrowings	
Net cash used in financing activities	
NET CHANGE IN CASH AND CASH EQUIVALENTS	**1,451**
Cash and cash equivalents at start of the year	4,332
Cash and cash equivalents at end of the year	**5,783**

The income statements shows the revenue earned and the costs incurred. The balance sheet shows changes in the amounts owed by customers and owed to suppliers – these changes reflect cash receipts from customers and cash payments to suppliers:

OMEGA TRADING COMPANY LIMITED

$000's omitted

Payments made to suppliers	
Cost of goods sold to customers	(77,160)
Increase in stock ($36,850 to $41,795)	(5,215)
Increase in amount owed to suppliers ($6,013 to $6,765)	752
Payments made to suppliers	**(81,623)**

Indirect method of calculating operating cash flow

OMEGA TRADING COMPANY LIMITED

Indirect method of calculating cash generated from activities

$000's omitted	2015
Operating profit	13,340
Depreciation	4,000

(Increase)/decrease in stocks	(5,215)
(Increase)/decrease in debtors	(2,027)
(Decrease)/increase in creditors	752
(Increase)/decrease in working capital	(6,491)
Cash generated from operations	**10,849**
Interest charges paid	(750)
Tax paid	(3,148)
Net cash generated from operating activities	**6,951**

The indirect method starts with the operating profit for the period. A depreciation charge is purely an accounting entry and never involves the exchange of cash, so this type of non-cash item must be ignored in any calculation of cash flow. A depreciation charge has been included as a cost in calculating the operating profit, so it is added back to the operating profit to eliminate it from the cash flow calculation. Amortisation and impairment charges are similar adjustments to the balance sheet value of assets, and both, like depreciation, are non-cash items.

Adjustments are then made to the operating profit calculated on an accruals basis, to reflect the effect on cash flow of changes in the level of the working capital.

Understanding working capital

Figure 6.1 illustrates how, in a business that buys and sells finished products, shareholders' funds are injected into the business in the form of cash. Some of the cash will be used to buy stock for sale, so reducing the amount of cash held. When stock is sold on credit terms to the company's customers, the amount of inventory available will be reduced but the amount invoiced to the customer will not immediately be paid. The company is now funding debtors (also referred to as receivables), the name given to the free loans made to customers in the form of trade credit. When customers eventually settle their invoices this is converted back into cash. This circulation process is referred to as the trade cycle.

Figure 6.1

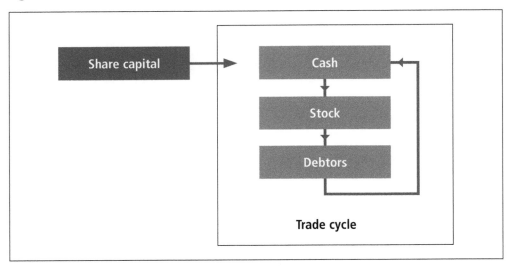

Trade credit (also referred to as trade payables) refers to the amount owed to the company's suppliers who have provided goods or services on trade credit. This represents an additional free source of funds for the business. At the end of the credit period allowed by the supplier, outstanding supplier invoices must be settled in cash and the funds remitted to the creditor, as shown in Figure 6.2.

Figure 6.2

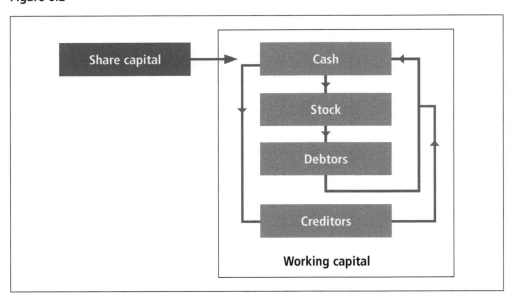

Working capital is the company's circulating capital, comprising cash, stock, debtors and creditors. Working capital is important because it has to be funded. When the level and composition of working capital changes, this has a direct effect on cash flow. Increases in inventory and debtors will reduce the level of cash, but a reduction in these working capital components will increase the amount of cash available. Further, an increase in the level of creditors will increase the level of cash, and vice versa.

The level of working capital is directly affected by changes in sales volumes. Inventory levels will increase in anticipation of the sales increase and customer credit levels will also increase when sales have been made. Working capital levels may also be affected by changes in stock holding policy, supply chain terms and trade credit terms.

The working capital cycle measures the average length of time between paying suppliers for goods and services provided and receiving payment from the company's customers. These different measures were described in Chapter 3.

Working capital cycle	days
Average inventory turnover period	X
+ Average time for customers to pay	X
- Average credit period from suppliers	(X)
= Working capital cycle	X

Working capital cycles may vary significantly depending on the type of industry. In the service sector, little or no inventory is needed so the time between paying suppliers and receiving cash from customers is likely to be quite short. But manufacturing companies often hold large inventories of raw materials and intermediate products, and most sales are on credit. In this case, the working capital cycle will be considerably longer. The working capital cycle is one of the key factors that determine how much cash is required by a company to operate and compete effectively. It also has a significant effect on the amount of funding the company will require in order to grow the business.

When working capital is optimised and the circulation process operates smoothly, a business may maintain a constant level of sales without requiring additional funds. But if the company aims to grow sales revenue it will be necessary to increase the amount of working capital, and additional funding may be needed to finance this expansion.

Direct versus indirect method of calculating operating cash flow

The difference between these two methods may appear to be largely presentational, but they each represent different approaches to framing a cash flow calculation – viewing the task from two different perspectives. The indirect approach highlights the impact of changes in working capital on cash flow. In many kinds of business this can have a significant effect. In companies where working capital is not actively managed and monitored, this may leave the firm exposed to pressure on its cash resources and, in the most severe cases, insolvency.

Investing activities

Many businesses make periodic major investments in:

- Purchasing physical assets, such as property, plant, equipment and vehicles.

- Acquiring non-physical, so called intangible assets, such as investing in brands and software exploitation rights.

- Buying companies.

Although leasing has become a popular means by which to obtain the use of plant and equipment, for many companies these types of investing activities still require access to significant cash funds. However, cash may be generated from investing activities when redundant businesses or obsolete assets are sold.

Financing activities

Inward cash flows in this category typically include:

- Funds received from the issue of new share capital.

- Funds borrowed from a bank.

- In the case of large public companies, funds from the issue of corporate bonds.

There may also be cash outflows in the form of:

- Loan repayments.

- Redemption of corporate bonds.

- Payments under capital leases.

- Dividend payments to shareholders.

Forecasting cash flow

There are two approaches to making cash flow forecasts. They differ in the way that they deal with operating cash flow, using either the direct or indirect method.

Direct method of cash flow forecasting

The direct method forecasts operating cash flow by predicting the cash receipts and cash payments for each future forecast period. Financial data from the company's purchase and sales accounting ledgers can usually be used to make fairly accurate cash flow predictions for periods of up to six to eight weeks. Outside of this timeframe, recent cash flow history may be used to calculate average receipts and payments, and to identify the timing of significant cash flow items.

But care must be taken to allow for any seasonal factors that might make a significant difference to the level of receipts and payments. The direct method is less helpful for predicting cash flow in a dynamic environment; for example, when the business is going through a period of growth or contraction. Under these conditions it is difficult to predict changes in working capital levels using the direct method. The approach to forecasting investing and financing activities is the same under both the indirect and direct method.

Direct cash flow forecast example

OMEGA TRADING COMPANY LIMITED

Cash flow forecast for 2016

$000's omitted	JAN	FEB	MAR
Operating cash receipts:			
Credit sales prior month	3,200	2,800	3,400
Credit sales two months prior	5,100	4,800	5,200
Cash sales	1,200	1,400	1,100
	9,500	9,000	9,700
Operating cash payments:			
Payment for current month purchases	(2,700)	(2,800)	(2,500)
Payment for purchases in current month	(4,300)	(4,100)	(4,400)

Payment for rent			(3,000)
Payment for wages and salaries	(1,200)	(1,200)	(1,400)
	(8,200)	(8,100)	(11,300)
Interest charges paid	(150)		
Tax paid			(1,500)
Net cash generated from operating activities	1,150	900	(3,100)
Purchase of plant and equipment		(1,500)	
Net cash used in investing activities		(1,500)	
Net cash used in financing activities			
NET CHANGE IN CASH AND CASH EQUIVALENTS	1,150	(600)	(3,100)
Cash and cash equivalents at start of the period	5,783	6,933	6,333
Cash and cash equivalents at end of the period	**6,933**	**6,333**	**3,233**

Indirect method of cash flow forecasting

The indirect method calculates operating cash flow by predicting operating profit and changes in the level of working capital components based on sales forecasts. This approach works by identifying the relationship between the level of sales activity and its impact on gross margins and working capital components. These relationships can be used as the basis for inputs into a financial model that can be used to measure the effect of changes in sales revenue and other assumptions on operating cash flow. The cash flow forecasting model uses this indirect approach.

Input assumptions for the Cash Flow Forecasting Model

The sales revenue forecast assumption is the primary driver for the cash flow model. The cost of goods sold assumption is expressed as a percentage of the sales revenue, because these costs generally increase in proportion to the sales revenue. In some organisations, sales and distribution costs may also vary to some degree in relation to sales revenue –

but in this model these costs are assumed to be fixed and independent of sales revenue levels, as are the administration costs. The administration cost assumption excludes depreciation charges and any other non-cash items like amortisation (a charge similar to depreciation that reflects a reduction in the value of intangible assets like brands and other forms of intellectual property).

Loan interest and capital payments can be predicted based on the repayment schedule set out in relevant loan agreements. Corporation tax is based on business profits, but cash tax payments in any period are likely to relate to profits from an earlier period and will be based on tax authority payment schedules. Input assumptions include specific prediction of tax cash payments, rather than calculating the tax payment as a percentage of operating cash flow for each forecast period.

Screenshot 6.1

	A	B	C	D	E
1	**ASSUMPTIONS**		JAN	FEB	MAR
2	**Operating cash flow assumptions**				
3	Sales revenue - £000's		3,000	2,700	3,800
4	% cost of goods sold		64%	64%	64%
5	Sales and distribution costs - £000's		(200)	(200)	(250)
6	Administration costs - £000's		(600)	(600)	(600)
7	Loan interest paid - £000's				
8	Corporation tax paid - £000's				
9					
10	**Working capital assumptions**				
11	Days' sales in stock		85	85	90
12	Debtor days outstanding		50	50	50
13	Creditor days		35	35	35
14	Opening balances 1st January:				
15	Stock - £000's	350			
16	Debtors - £000's	330			
17	Creditors - £000's	200			
18	Cash - £000's	520			
19					
20	**Investment assumptions**				
21	Purchases of plant and equipment - £000's		(750)		
22	Proceeds from disposal of assets - £000's				
23					
24	**Financing assumptions**				
25	Loan funds received - £000's				
26	Loan repayments - £000's				
27	Dividends paid - £000's				
28					
29					
30					

INPUT | CASH FLOW FORECAST

The input assumptions used for the working capital components allow the forecast model to establish a dynamic link between sales revenue and the level of stock and trade credit needed to support it. Chapter 3 explained how working capital efficiency ratios could be used to calculate: the number of days' sales outstanding in debtors; the number of days' sales represented in inventory; and the number of days worth of sales represented in creditors. The ratios were calculated as:

$$Days'\ sales\ outstanding\ (DSO)\ =\ \frac{Trade\ debtors}{Sales\ revenue} \times 365$$

$$Days'\ sales\ in\ inventory\ (DSI)\ =\ \frac{Inventory\ at\ cost}{Cost\ of\ goods\ sold} \times 365$$

$$Creditor\ days\ or\ days'\ payable\ outstanding\ (DPO)$$
$$=\ \frac{Creditors}{Cost\ of\ goods\ sold} \times 365$$

DSO, DSI and DPO can be used as input assumptions and used in conjunction with the sales revenue prediction to make a forecast for working capital component levels. Changes in net working capital can then be calculated for the purpose of making an indirect calculation of operating cash flow; for example, by modifying the DSO ratio calculation a trade debtors forecast can be made as:

$$\frac{DSO\ \times\ Sales\ revenue}{365}\ =\ Trade\ debtors$$

A similar approach may be used to forecast inventory and creditors, but in these cases the cost of sales will be used for the calculation, rather than sales revenue. Assumptions include the working capital balances at the start of the year so that the increase or decrease in net working capital in January may be calculated.

The operating cash flow section of the forecast

This extract from the cash flow forecast model shows the formulae used to generate the indirect operating cash flow forecast for January, and how the cost of goods sold and the working capital components are dynamically linked to the sales revenue forecast. The same approach is used for each month of the forecast.

Screenshot 6.2

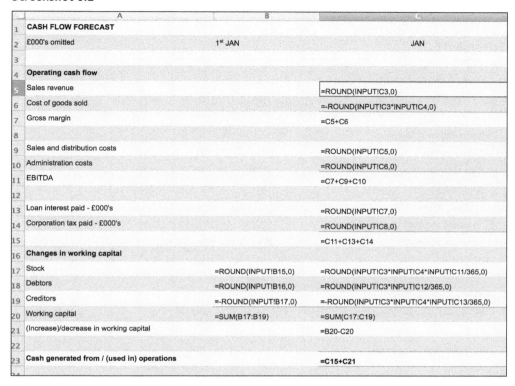

	A	B	C
1	CASH FLOW FORECAST		
2	£000's omitted	1st JAN	JAN
3			
4	Operating cash flow		
5	Sales revenue		=ROUND(INPUT!C3,0)
6	Cost of goods sold		=-ROUND(INPUT!C3*INPUT!C4,0)
7	Gross margin		=C5+C6
8			
9	Sales and distribution costs		=ROUND(INPUT!C5,0)
10	Administration costs		=ROUND(INPUT!C6,0)
11	EBITDA		=C7+C9+C10
12			
13	Loan interest paid - £000's		=ROUND(INPUT!C7,0)
14	Corporation tax paid - £000's		=ROUND(INPUT!C8,0)
15			=C11+C13+C14
16	Changes in working capital		
17	Stock	=ROUND(INPUT!B15,0)	=ROUND(INPUT!C3*INPUT!C4*INPUT!C11/365,0)
18	Debtors	=ROUND(INPUT!B16,0)	=ROUND(INPUT!C3*INPUT!C12/365,0)
19	Creditors	=-ROUND(INPUT!B17,0)	=-ROUND(INPUT!C3*INPUT!C4*INPUT!C13/365,0)
20	Working capital	=SUM(B17:B19)	=SUM(C17:C19)
21	(Increase)/decrease in working capital		=B20-C20
22			
23	Cash generated from / (used in) operations		=C15+C21

The model uses the Excel ROUND function for each of the calculations to ensure that the forecast is maintained at £000 accuracy and to avoid errors of addition when calculating intermediate totals in the forecast. The function takes the form:

ROUND(number or cell reference(s), number of decimal places required)

EBITDA (earnings before interest, taxation, depreciation and amortisation)

EBITDA has become a common measure of operating profit before non-cash items. It represents the operating cash flow generated before adjusting for changes in the level of working capital. In industry sectors like capital asset leasing, where working capital may be relatively minimal, EBITDA is a good proxy for operating cash flow before interest and tax payments and the effect on cash flow of changes in working capital.

The output from the operating cash flow section of the forecast

Screenshot 6.3

	A	B	C	D	E
1	CASH FLOW FORECAST				
2	£000's omitted	1ˢᵗ JAN	JAN	FEB	MAR
3					
4	**Operating cash flow**				
5	Sales revenue		3,000	2,700	3,800
6	Cost of goods sold		(1,920)	(1,728)	(2,432)
7	Gross margin		1,080	972	1,368
8					
9	Sales and distribution costs		(200)	(200)	(250)
10	Administration costs		(600)	(600)	(600)
11	EBITDA		280	172	518
12					
13	Loan interest paid - £000's				
14	Corporation tax paid - £000's				
15			280	172	518
16	**Changes in working capital**				
17	Stock	350	447	402	600
18	Debtors	330	411	370	521
19	Creditors	(200)	(184)	(166)	(233)
20	Working capital	480	674	606	888
21	(Increase)/decrease in working capital		(194)	68	(282)
22					
23	**Cash generated from / (used in) operations**		**86**	**240**	**236**

Forecasting with strong seasonal sales patterns

Seasonal sales patterns are more marked in some industries than in others; this example does not show particularly strong seasonal sales. In companies where there are strong seasonal sales, inventory levels will tend to increase in the months prior to the high sales periods. The cash flow forecasting model takes a simple approach. It calculates monthly working capital components based on the sales revenue and the cost of sales prediction for the same month. If you are making a cash flow forecast for a business with particularly strong seasonality it may be necessary to manually increase the days sales in inventory and creditor days in the month(s) leading up to the peak sales months.

Investing activities and financing activities

Screenshot 6.4

	A	B	C
22			
23	Cash generated from / (used in) operations		=C15+C21
24			
25	Investing activities		
26	Purchases of plant and equipment		=ROUND(INPUT!C21,0)
27	Proceeds from disposal of assets		=ROUND(INPUT!C22,0)
28	Cash generated from / (used in) investing activities		=C26+C27
29			
30	Financing activities		
31	Loan funds received		=ROUND(INPUT!C25,0)
32	Loan repayments		=ROUND(INPUT!C26,0)
33	Dividend payments		=ROUND(INPUT!C27,0)
34	Cash generated from / (used in) investing activities		=SUM(C31:C33)
35			
36	NET CASH FLOW		=C23+C28+C34
37			
38	CASH BALANCE	=ROUND(INPUT!B18,0)	=B38+C36

This extract from the cash flow forecasting model shows the formulae used to generate the cash flow forecast for investing and financing activities. In each case, the input assumption has been taken from the INPUT sheet without further calculation.

The output from the investing and financing sections

Screenshot 6.5

	A	B	C	D	E
1	CASH FLOW FORECAST				
2	£000's omitted	1st JAN	JAN	FEB	MAR
23	Cash generated from / (used in) operations		86	240	236
24					
25	Investing activities				
26	Purchases of plant and equipment			(750)	
27	Proceeds from disposal of assets				
28	Cash generated from / (used in) investing activities			(750)	
29					
30	Financing activities				
31	Loan funds received				
32	Loan repayments				
33	Dividend payments				
34	Cash generated from / (used in) investing activities				
35					
36	NET CASH FLOW		86	(510)	236
37					
38	CASH BALANCE	520	606	96	332

Using the Cash Flow Forecasting Model to test the impact of risk on cash flow

Conventional forecasts aim to produce a single definitive forecast, often focusing, at a very detailed level, on the outputs from the forecast. The Cash Flow Forecasting Model focuses on a small number of key inputs and uses identified causal relationships, such as that between sales revenue and working capital, to generate the output. The dynamic nature of the model, and the structure and approach used in building it, allows multiple versions of the forecast to be quickly produced simply by changing one or more of the key driver assumptions.

This kind of approach offers two significant advantages. First, it allows managers and analysts to test the potential impact of various types of risks and uncertainties on the timing and quantum of the cash flows. For example, changing the cost of goods percentage assumption can test the impact of a change in the cost of raw materials caused by a price change or currency conversion rate change. Second, a *what if* approach can be applied to test the sensitivity of the firm's cash flow to changes in various input drivers.

For example, the model will reveal that in some businesses relatively small changes to the levels of inventory and customer credit terms can have a major impact on cash flow, perhaps even greater than the effect of a customer price increase. This provides a very powerful tool to help to focus attention on areas for action to improve cash flow.

The complete output section of the cash flow forecasting app

Screenshot 6.6

		1st JAN	JAN	FEB	MAR
1	**CASH FLOW FORECAST**				
2	£000's omitted	1st JAN	JAN	FEB	MAR
3					
4	**Operating cash flow**				
5	Sales revenue		3,000	2,700	3,800
6	Cost of goods sold		(1,920)	(1,728)	(2,432)
7	Gross margin		1,080	972	1,368
8					
9	Sales and distribution costs		(200)	(200)	(250)
10	Administration costs		(600)	(600)	(600)
11	EBITDA		280	172	518
12					
13	Loan interest paid - £000's				
14	Corporation tax paid - £000's				
15			280	172	518
16	**Changes in working capital**				
17	Stock	350	447	402	600
18	Debtors	330	411	370	521
19	Creditors	(200)	(184)	(166)	(233)
20	Working capital	480	674	606	888
21	(Increase)/decrease in working capital		(194)	68	(282)
22					
23	**Cash generated from / (used in) operations**		86	240	236
24					
25	**Investing activities**				
26	Purchases of plant and equipment			(750)	
27	Proceeds from disposal of assets				
28	**Cash generated from / (used in) investing activities**			(750)	
29					
30	**Financing activities**				
31	Loan funds received				
32	Loan repayments				
33	Dividend payments				
34	**Cash generated from / (used in) investing activities**				
35					
36	**NET CASH FLOW**		86	(510)	236
37					
38	**CASH BALANCE**	520	606	96	332

Chapter 7

Model 4: Pricing and Profit

Harvard Business School Professor, Michael Porter, argues that the aim of business strategy is to use an advantage to create a unique mix of value for customers that will generate the sales revenue and profit with which the enterprise creates value for its shareholders.

Studies show that customers rarely perceive and measure value purely in terms of price, but rather based on their own evaluation of the benefits they receive from a product or service in relation to the price they are asked to pay for it. In other words, customers are happy when they believe that they *got what they paid for*. This explains, for example, how both BMW and Toyota can coexist as profitable motor manufacturers, each offering a unique combination of price and benefits that meet the needs of different sets of customers. For this reason, decisions about pricing for products and services should be primarily based on competitive market forces and customer expectations and attitudes.

Profit is what remains after all of the costs of producing and delivering a firm's products or services have been deducted from the sales revenue they have generated. Profit is one of the key measures of shareholder value and, as an important driver of operational cash flow, a vital element in the survival and long-term success of any business. So, although customer and market considerations must always inform pricing decisions, it is also important to ensure that the price charged at the volume sold will generate sufficient revenue to cover the relevant costs and produce a profit.

The Pricing and Profit Model

- **Users:** A financial analyst or financial planning manager would typically use this financial model to analyse and understand the impact of price changes on gross margin, break-even point and profit.

- **Purpose:** The model has two modules. The first assesses the impact of individual product price changes on the gross margin generated by the product to assist in price decision-making. The second part calculates the break-even point for a business and uses a Cost-Volume-Profit (CVP) chart to help in analysing and understanding the organisation's cost structure and profitability at various sales levels.

- **Outputs:** The output is shown on three Excel worksheets: a price change analysis worksheet; a CVP analysis worksheet; and a worksheet for the dynamic CVP chart.

- **Inputs:** There is one Excel Input worksheet combining two sets of inputs for the price change model and for the CVP analysis.

- **Calculations:** The calculations for the price change analysis are incorporated into the output report. A separate Excel worksheet is used to calculate the data to plot the CVP chart.

- **Design:** Assumptions are entered into the INPUT sheet. Calculation and output is combined in the PRICE CHECK sheet. Data for the CVP chart is calculated in the CVP CALCULATION sheet and the output is shown in the CVP ANALYSIS sheet. Refer to the Excel workbook: PRICING AND PROFIT MODEL.xlsx

Topic refresher – understanding pricing and profit

A company can be viewed as a system for creating value for customers and shareholders. It uses resources in the form of raw materials, human expertise and machinery to carry out the processes and activities that produce outputs in the form of the products and services that create value for customers. Value is created for shareholders in the form of profit, created when the revenue generated from the sale of the outputs is greater than the cost of the resources used in carrying out the organisation's processes and activities that created the outputs.

Figure 7.1

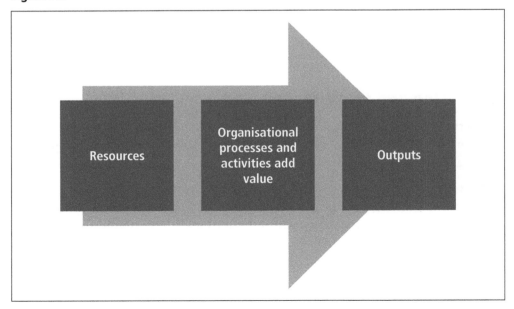

It is vital at a strategic level to understand how the company creates value from its operational activities, and the way that they are linked together. It is also important to understand how different products, services and customers create value. While it is usually straightforward to calculate the sales revenue generated by different products, it is often more problematic to calculate the total costs of producing them. This is because of the way that different kinds of costs behave, illustrated by the example below.

Acme Widget Company

The company buys and sells widgets. In the current year, the firm expects to sell 12m units at £1 each and the widgets cost £0.70 each. The office rent, salaries and other overhead costs are expected to be £2.4m for the year.

Acme Widget Company	
Sales	£12,000,000
Cost of sales	(£8,400,000)
Gross margin	£3,600,000
Overhead costs	(£2,400,000)
Operating profit	**£1,200,000**

The profit statement shows that the company makes an operating profit of £1.2m on expected sales of £12m – but what would be the operating result on sales of 10m units? The widgets are sold for £1 each, so it is straightforward to calculate that the revenue will be £10m, but a cost forecast can be made only when there is a clear understanding of how the firm's costs behave when sales levels change.

Cost behaviour describes how costs change in response to changes in the level of sales or production. Fixed costs are those costs that are unaffected by changes in volume across a wide range of output. Rent, HR, IT and many other kinds of costs, normally referred to as overhead costs, are examples of fixed costs. Eventually the business may grow to a point where some of these costs will show a step increase to cope with greater organisational demands; for example, if the firm has to rent a larger warehouse. Costs will then remain fixed at this new level so long as the firm operates within the new level of capacity. In the Acme Widget example the overhead costs would be fixed.

Variable costs are those costs that vary directly with the level of activity. They include product raw material costs, finished goods purchase costs and may, sometimes, include freight costs if they are charged on a unit basis or as a percentage of sales revenue. In the Acme Widget Company example the cost price of the widgets is variable. The Cost-Volume-Profit chart below illustrates the relationship between fixed and variable costs.

Figure 7.2

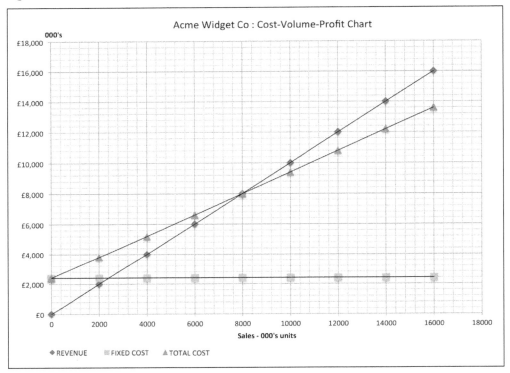

Interpreting the Cost-Volume-Profit (CVP) chart

The fixed cost line plots the annual overhead costs that are fixed at £2.4m for any volume of sales within the company's existing capacity. The total cost line plots total costs, comprising fixed costs of £2.4m per year and variable costs of £0.70 per unit. So, if zero units are sold, total costs will be equal to the fixed costs and, thereafter, the total costs will increase at the rate of £0.70 per unit sold. For example, the CVP chart shows that when 6m units are sold, the total costs equal £6.6m, which is comprised of £2.4m in fixed costs and £4.2m (6m x £0.70) in variable costs. The revenue line plots sales revenue increasing at the rate of £1 per unit from zero to £16m, at the point where 16m units have been sold.

Gross margin and break-even point

The key point on the CVP chart is to be found at 8m units, where the total cost and revenue lines intersect. In other words, the point at which total costs are exactly equal to sales revenue. At this point, the company has achieved break-even. When sales are below 8m units, the total costs will exceed revenue and the company will make a loss. When sales exceed 8m units, the company will make a profit.

Acme Widget Company	
Sales	£8,000,000
Cost of sales	(£5,600,000)
Gross margin	£2,400,000
Overhead costs	(£2,400,000)
Operating profit	**£0**

The revised profit statement (above) shows that at sales of 8m units the total costs are equal to sales revenue. Looking at this from a different perspective, this profit statement also demonstrates that in order to achieve break-even, the business must generate sufficient gross margin to pay for the fixed costs. This approach highlights two realities that can provide the basis of effective business decision-making. It is gross margin rather than sales revenue that represents the company's real income, and profit is maximised when the margin on sales is maximised. In the Acme Widget Company example, the gross margin per unit is £0.30, calculated as:

Selling price per unit	£1.00
Variable cost per unit	£0.70
Gross margin per unit	£0.30

The break-even point can then be calculated using this formula:

$$Break-even\ point\ =\ \frac{Fixed\ costs}{Gross\ margin\ per\ unit}$$

In the Acme Widget Company example:

$$\frac{£2,400,000}{£0.30} = 8m \ units$$

The break-even point may also be calculated in terms of the sales revenue level at which break-even is achieved. This is calculated as:

$$Break-even \ sales \ value = \frac{Fixed \ costs}{Gross \ margin \ percentage}$$

Gross margin percentage is calculated as:

$$Gross \ margin \ percentage = \frac{Gross \ margin \ per \ unit}{Selling \ price \ per \ unit} \times 100$$

So in the Acme Widget Company example:

$$\frac{Gross \ margin \ per \ unit}{Selling \ price \ per \ unit} = \frac{£0.30}{£1.00} = 30\%$$

Break-even sales value can then be calculated as:

$$\frac{Fixed \ costs}{Gross \ margin \ percentage} = \frac{£2,400,000}{0.3} = £8,000,000$$

Note how the gross margin percentage is expressed as a decimal for the calculation.

Gross margin and pricing

Although pricing decisions should be based primarily on competitive market considerations, the gross margin and break-even relationship provides the basis to confirm that the market price will produce an acceptable profit for the company.

The Acme Widget Company is an example of a company that buys and sells a single product. The Omega Trading Company buys and sells a number of different products. The company's profit statement is shown below:

Omega Trading Company Profit Statement		
Sales	£12,000,000	100%
Variable costs	(£7,200,00)	(60)%
Gross margin	£4,800,000	40%
Fixed costs	(£3,000,000)	(25)%
Operating profit	£1,800,000	15%

The Omega Trading Company's £3m fixed costs represent 25% of £12m sales revenue so, at this level of turnover, the company will need to achieve an overall gross margin of 25% to cover the fixed costs, and so achieve break-even. The firm will, of course, be aiming to make a profit and may have set a strategic goal to create shareholder value based on Return on Net Assets (Chapter 3). If this goal were dependent on achieving a profit margin of 15% on sales then the company would need to generate an overall gross margin of 40% on £12m sales in order to achieve an operating profit at this level. Companies typically sell a number of products with different levels of gross margin percentage, but a specified target would allow them to focus on achieving the appropriate overall average.

Pricing and sales volume decisions

While it is true that pricing decisions should be made, primarily, by reference to market and competitive factors, many marketing and sales managers focus purely on the selling price when negotiating prices and discounts with customers – without considering the impact of these prices changes on gross margin. No price or discount changes should be agreed without first assessing the impact on gross margin. What may seem like a good opportunity from a price and volume point of view may have a disproportionately adverse effect on gross margin. Consider the following:

A company sells a product for £10 per unit and the variable cost of the product is £7.50. In a typical year the firm sells 10,000 units. The sales manager believes that a 10% price reduction would lead to a 20% increase in annual sales. Good deal or bad?

	Before	After	
Selling price per unit	£10.00	£9.00	-10%
Variable cost per unit	£7.50	£7.50	
Gross margin per unit	£2.50	£1.50	-40%

Annual sales units	10,000	12,000	+20%
Gross margin on sales	£25,000	£18,000	-28%

To those unfamiliar with the concept of gross margin, it may seem like an attractive proposition to reduce the selling price of a product by 10% in return for a 20% increase in sales volumes. The analysis above shows that the effect of this price change is to reduce both the selling price and the gross margin by £1 and, although this represents only a fairly modest 10% reduction in price, it results in a very significant 40% reduction in gross margin (the firm's real income).

The expected 20% increase in sales volume would increase annual sales to 12,000 units, but at the lower unit gross margin this generates gross margin on sales of £18,000, a reduction of 28% compared to the £25,000 margin at the old price.

The company would have to sell 16,667 units to generate £25,000 margin – this is an increase of 67% over the 10,000 annual units typically sold at the original price!

Similarly, when a product price increase is considered purely on the basis of price and volume, a false conclusion may be drawn. For example, let's say the sales manager has assessed that a 10% price increase would lead to a 25% reduction in sales volume; quite a significant reduction in volume, but what would be the effect on unit gross margin and margin on sales?

	Before	**After**	
Selling price per unit	£10.00	£11.00	+10%
Variable cost per unit	£7.50	£7.50	
Gross margin per unit	£2.50	£3.50	+40%
Annual sales units	10,000	7,500	-25%
Gross margin on sales	£25,000	£26,250	+5%

The 10% price increase in price produces a £1 increase in both the price and gross margin per unit and this represents a healthy 40% increase in the gross margin per unit. If sales volumes fall by 25% to 7,500 units per year the margin on sales actually increases to £26,250, an increase of 5% over the margin on sales at the old price.

The limitations of this approach

Making strategic decisions about product design and pricing depends on insights into the profit generated by the company's different products. The profit generated by any product or service is a function of its price and the full costs incurred in producing, selling and distributing it. In other words, not just the variable cost of the product, but also any fixed costs incurred. In businesses where the processes involved in producing, selling and distributing different kinds of products are broadly the same, the resulting fixed overhead costs incurred will also be the same. In this case there is no particular benefit in attempting to apportion the fixed overhead between these different products – the gross margin approach provides a good basis for making decisions about pricing and profit maximisation. This makes the marginal approach eminently suitable for retail businesses and those types of manufacturing companies where different types of product follow a broadly standard manufacturing process.

However, there are some situations where overhead costs are not incurred evenly across the firm's different products and, in these circumstances, the marginal approach to decision-making may not be the most appropriate because it makes no attempt to establish an accurate full cost for each specific kind of product. Traditional absorption costing methods aim to address this shortcoming by apportioning the overhead costs directly incurred in production (for example, engineering costs in setting up machines and production energy costs) across each unit of production by means of a simple volume-related measure – such as direct labour hours used, or production machine hours used.

These simple overhead apportionment techniques obscure the real cost of different kinds of products by assuming that the activities the organisation carries out in making its various types of product are consumed evenly in proportion to the volume of production, but this is not always the case. It is quite common to find that companies make a combination of high-volume products that are relatively straightforward to manufacture, and low-volume specialised products that are more complex to produce and account for a disproportionate amount of time involved in carrying out various production activities – such as setting up and dismounting machine tools and jigs, etc. In these firms, an Activity Based Costing (ABC) approach may provide more meaningful insights, albeit on the basis of a rather more complicated costing system.

The Pricing and Profit Model workbook

The workbook has five worksheets comprising: an input sheet; two output sheets; a worksheet to calculate the data with which to plot the CVP chart; and a separate sheet for the CVP chart itself. The structure of the model is shown in Figure 7.3.

Figure 7.3

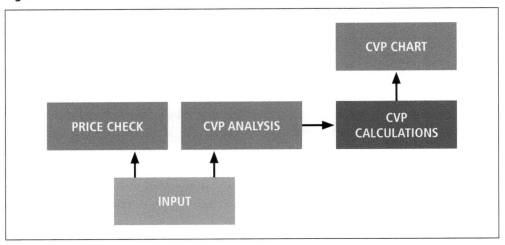

Input worksheet for the Pricing and Profit Model

Screenshot 7.1

	A	B	C	D
1	**UNIT PRICE CHANGE ASSUMPTIONS**			
2		Current		New
3	Selling price per unit	£10.00		£9.00
4	Variable cost per unit	£7.50		£7.50
5	Annual sales units	10,000		12,000
6				
7	**COST-VOLUME-PROFIT ASSUMPTIONS**			
8	Annual sales revenue	£3,000,000		
9	Annual sales units	317,236		
10	Variable cost of sales	£2,000,000		
11	Annual fixed costs	£750,000		
12				

The unit price change assumptions require the current and proposed unit selling price of the product to be entered, along with the variable cost per unit (which would normally be the same for both the existing and new selling price). The third input is for average annual sales units at the current price and the projected or expected annual sales under the new selling price.

The Cost-Volume-Profit assumptions are the annual sales revenue for the company, the annual sales units, the annual variable cost of sales and the annual fixed costs.

The input assumptions in both sections should all be entered as positive numbers.

The Price Check Analysis Model

Screenshot 7.2

	A	B	C	D	E	F
1	**PRICE CHECK**					
2		Current price		New price		% change
4	Price per unit	£10.00		£9.00		(10.0)%
5	Variable cost per unit	£(7.50)		£(7.50)		
6	Gross margin per unit	£2.50		£1.50		(40.0)%
7						
8	Annual sales	10,000		12,000		20.0%
9						
10	Margin on sales	£25,000		£18,000		(28.0)%
11						
12	Annual sales needed to achieve current margin			16,667		66.7%

The Price Check analysis calculates the impact of a proposed price change on the gross margin per unit and on the margin on sales. The model also calculates the annual sales volume required at the new price to achieve the same margin on sales that was achieved at the old price. The formulae for these calculations are shown in Screenshot 7.3.

Screenshot 7.3

	A	B	C	D	E	F
1	**PRICE CHECK**					
2		Current price		New price		% change
3						
4	Price per unit	=INPUT!B3		=INPUT!D3		=D4/B4-1
5	Variable cost per unit	=-INPUT!B4		=-INPUT!D4		
6	Gross margin per unit	=B4+B5		=D4+D5		=D6/B6-1
7						
8	Annual sales	=INPUT!B5		=INPUT!D5		=D8/B8-1
9						
10	Margin on sales	=B8*B6		=D8*D6		=D10/B10-1
11						
12	Annual sales needed to achieve current margin			=B10/D6		=D12/B8-1

The Cost-Volume-Profit Analysis Model

Screenshot 7.4

	A	B	C	D	E
1	**COST-VOLUME-PROFIT ANALYSIS**				
2		Annual		Average per unit	
3	Sales revenue	£3,000,000		£9.46	
4	Variable cost	(£2,000,000)		(£6.30)	
5	Gross margin	£1,000,000		£3.16	
6	Gross margin percentage			33.4%	
7					
8	Fixed costs	(£750,000)			
9					
10	Profit on actual sales	£250,000		£0.79	
11					
12	Break-even sales value	£2,245,253			
13	Break-even sales units	237,342			

The input assumption for annual sales units is used to calculate: the average price per unit; the variable cost per unit; the gross margin per unit; and the gross margin percentage. The model uses the resulting gross margin percentage and gross margin per unit to calculate the break-even sales value and break-even sales units. In cases where the variable costs are greater than the sales revenue, a negative gross margin is produced – making it impossible to achieve break-even at any sales level. In this case the model shows a zero value and a warning message instead of break-even sales value and break-even sales units. The formulae used in the CVP analysis are shown in Screenshot 7.5.

Screenshot 7.5

	A	B	C	D
1	COST-VOLUME-PROFIT ANALYSIS			
2		Annual		Average per unit
3	Sales revenue	=INPUT!B8		=ROUND(INPUT!B8/INPUT!B9,2)
4	Variable cost	=-INPUT!B10		=-ROUND(INPUT!B10/INPUT!B9,2)
5	Gross margin	=B3+B4		=D3+D4
6	Gross margin percentage			=D5/D3
7				
8	Fixed costs	=-INPUT!B11		
9				
10	Profit on actual sales	=B5+B8		=ROUND(B10/INPUT!B9,2)
11				
12	Break-even sales value	=IF(-B8/D6<=0,0,-ROUND(B8/D6,0))		=IF(B12=0,"Break-even cannot be calculated when gross margin is zero or negative","")
13	Break-even sales units	=IF(-B8/D5<=0,0,-ROUND(B8/D5,0))		

INPUT · PRICE CHECK · **CVP ANALYSIS** · CVP CHART · CVP CALCULATIONS · +

CVP calculations

The break-even data from the CVP Analysis worksheet is used in this worksheet to calculate an appropriate range of values with which to plot the annual sales units on the horizontal axis of the CVP chart. The sales revenues, fixed costs and total costs are calculated at each of these sales levels, and these are used to plot the three corresponding lines on the CVP chart.

Screenshot 7.6

	A	B	C	D
1	**COST-VOLUME-PROFIT DATA**			
2	SALES UNITS	REVENUE	FIXED COST	TOTAL COST
3	0	£0	£750,000	£750,000
4	118,671	£1,122,234	£750,000	£1,498,156
5	237,342	£2,244,468	£750,000	£2,246,312
6	317,236	£3,000,000	£750,000	£2,750,000
7	412,407	£3,900,000	£750,000	£3,350,000
8				

| INPUT | PRICE CHECK | CVP ANALYSIS | CVP CHART | CVP CALCULATIONS | + |

The sales units in cell A5 are the break-even sales units calculated in the CVP Analysis sheet – this effectively places the break-even point in the middle of the CVP chart. The actual annual sales units are taken from the Input sheet and used in either cell A4 or A6 of the chart calculations, depending on whether actual sales are less than or greater than the calculated break-even sales units.

Variable costs per unit are calculated from the assumptions for annual sales units and annual variable costs in the Input worksheet. In column D of the CVP calculation sheet, this is multiplied by the relevant sales unit values in column A to calculate variable costs. This is then added to the value for fixed costs in column C in order to calculate the total cost. The formulae are shown in Screenshot 7.7.

Screenshot 7.7

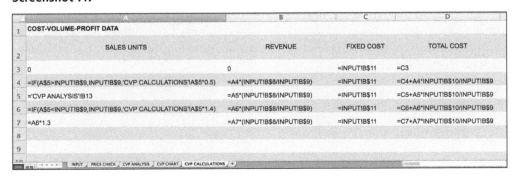

	A	B	C	D
1	COST-VOLUME-PROFIT DATA			
2	SALES UNITS	REVENUE	FIXED COST	TOTAL COST
3	0	0	=INPUT!B$11	=C3
4	=IF(A$5>INPUT!B$9,INPUT!B$9,'CVP CALCULATIONS'!A$5*0.5)	=A4*(INPUT!B$8/INPUT!B$9)	=INPUT!B$11	=C4+A4*INPUT!B$10/INPUT!B$9
5	='CVP ANALYSIS'!B13	=A5*(INPUT!B$8/INPUT!B$9)	=INPUT!B$11	=C5+A5*INPUT!B$10/INPUT!B$9
6	=IF(A$5<INPUT!B$9,INPUT!B$9,'CVP CALCULATIONS'!A$5*1.4)	=A6*(INPUT!B$8/INPUT!B$9)	=INPUT!B$11	=C6+A6*INPUT!B$10/INPUT!B$9
7	=A6*1.3	=A7*(INPUT!B$8/INPUT!B$9)	=INPUT!B$11	=C7+A7*INPUT!B$10/INPUT!B$9
8				
9				

| INPUT | PRICE CHECK | CVP ANALYSIS | CVP CHART | CVP CALCULATIONS | + |

The CVP chart

The CVP chart can now be plotted using the data from the CVP Calculations sheet. The first step is to highlight the data to be used, as shown in Screenshot 7.8.

Screenshot 7.8

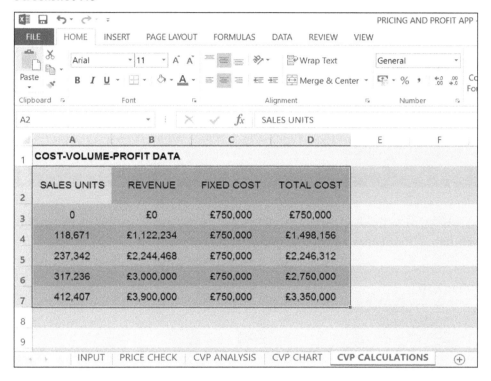

To produce a scatter diagram based on this data, click on the Insert ribbon and select the lined scatter diagram option from the dropdown menu.

Screenshot 7.9

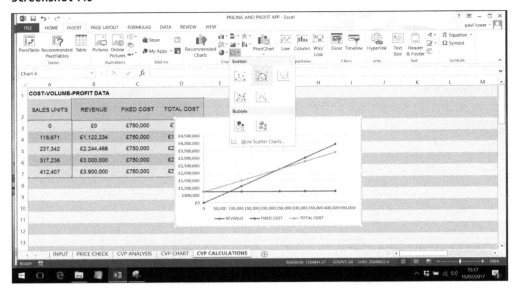

To move the chart to its own worksheet, click on the outside frame of the chart to select and then right click to open the dropdown menu.

Screenshot 7.10

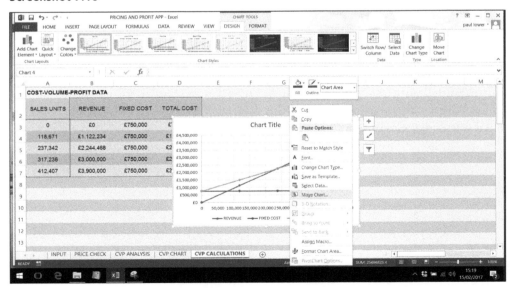

Choose the New Sheet option from the menu to move it to a new worksheet.

Screenshot 7.11

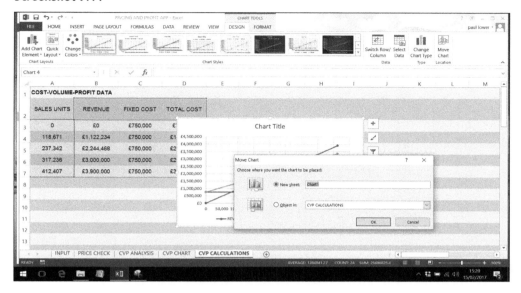

When the chart is moved to a new worksheet it becomes enlarged and the horizontal access units become more spaced and easier to read. Click on the outside frame of the chart and use the chart formatting and design tools to change the appearance of the chart as you prefer.

Screenshot 7.12

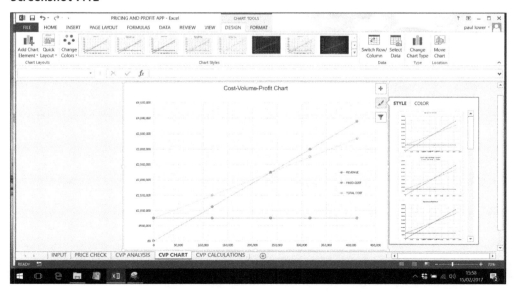

Chapter 8

Model 5:
Investment Decision

In simple terms, business investment can be considered as money spent on creating, developing, running or expanding an enterprise in the expectation of future returns. Many of the costs incurred in business, including research and development, staff training and marketing may be thought of as investment, even though from an accounting perspective they are deducted from sales revenue to calculate profit for the period in which they are incurred.

Capital investment, by comparison, typically involves significant cash outflows during an initial development phase followed by cash inflows in subsequent years as the investment project is brought to full productivity and reaches its maximum income generating potential. In many industries, for example petrochemicals and oil and gas, capital investment in various kinds of plant and processing equipment is a regular and recurring feature of business. Yet even in the largest global firms, access to finance is ultimately limited and, since it is impossible to undertake all capital investment projects, some kind of appraisal tool is needed with which to choose between them: based on the outflow of funds required to make the investment; the subsequent cash flows as a result of the investment; and the degree of risk that is perceived to be attached to the investment. There are three common approaches to capital investment appraisal, as detailed below.

The accounting rate of return method expresses annual profit generated from the project as a percentage of the initial investment cost. The appeal of this approach lies in its simplicity and its similarity to the ROI concept, but it is a profit-based method and ignores project cash flows. The preference for using cash flow rather than profit in business decision-making has already been discussed above. Being a percentage approach, the comparative size of competing projects is ignored. This method also places no significance on the timing of the project inflows – in other words, the so-called *time value* of money.

The payback method calculates the time taken for the project cash inflow to pay back the initial investment – an easy to understand concept that has the advantage of using project cash flows rather than profit, and allowing easy comparison of different investment opportunities. In the many companies where access to finance is constrained, the payback period may be an important consideration in the selection of investment projects. Other companies, for example, in the oil and gas sector, use this method as an initial *rule of thumb* indicator of project viability before embarking on a detailed economic analysis based on full project cash flows. The major drawback of relying wholly on this approach is that it ignores cash flows that take place after the payback point, and also disregards the time value of all of the project cash flows.

The discounted cash flow method is based on calculating the value today of all of the incremental free cash flows generated over the whole life of the project. The approach is specifically designed to reflect the time value of future cash flows. This method is the most common approach to capital investment appraisal in business and is the approach used for the Investment Decision Model.

The Investment Decision Model

- **Users:** A financial analyst, investment manager or project manager would typically use this financial model to make a comparative appraisal of various kinds of investment opportunities.

- **Purpose:** The model uses a discounted cash flow (DCF) approach, using Excel functions to calculate the net present value (NPV) and internal rate of return (IRR) of a project based on the cash benefits and costs over its whole life.

- **Outputs:** The output is in the form of a two-stage DCF analysis used to calculate a detailed cash flow analysis for a discrete period of five years and, in the second stage, a terminal project value based on the discounted value of the remaining cash flows.

- **Inputs:** There is one Excel Input worksheet for the assumptions for project cash flows, project life, terminal asset value and discount factor.

- **Calculations:** The calculations for DCF analysis are incorporated in to the DCF analysis output report.

- **Design:** Assumptions are entered into the INPUT sheet; calculation and output is combined in the DCF ANALYSIS sheet. The key output information, in the form of the project NPV and IRR, are repeated on the INPUT sheet so that the effect of any changes in the assumptions can be easily assessed.

Topic refresher – discounted cash flow and capital investment decisions

Most people, if offered the choice between receiving a significant sum of money today or in one year's time, would prefer to receive the cash now. There are several reasons why people express this time preference for cash: it will not be exposed to the risk of inflation; it can be invested to earn a return; or it can be spent and enjoyed. Any uncertainty over whether the cash will be paid is eliminated when it is received.

The interest concept is based on the premise that people should receive some form of compensation when they give up the use of their money for a period. Having done so, they have lost the opportunity to spend or invest it elsewhere, and have taken on the risk of non-repayment. The example below illustrates how compound interest is calculated on an initial deposit of £1,000 with annual 10% interest.

Year 1	Principal invested	£1,000
	Interest at 10%	£100
	Balance at end of year 1	£1,100
Year 2	Interest at 10%	£110
	Balance at end of year 2	£1,210

In the first year interest is calculated at 10% on the £1,000 principal invested. In mathematical terms we can say that interest is calculated as Pr, when P is the principal and r is the rate of interest. When the interest is added to the principal, the year 1 the balance becomes $P + Pr$ and this can be further simplified to $P(1+r)$. In the example, £1,000 x $(1 + 0.10)$ = £1,100.

Year 2 interest is calculated at 10% on the £1,100 balance at the start of the year; when the year 2 interest is added to this the year 2 balance is equal to $P(1+r)(1+r)$, which can be simplified to $P(1+r)^2$. This formula can be generalised so that the balance after n years can be calculated as $P(1+r)^n$ and we can then express the relationship between present value (PV) and future value (FV) as:

$$FV = PV(1+r)^n$$

In the above example, FV = £1,000$(1+ 0.10)^2$ so FV = £1,000 x 1.21 = £1,210

In the situation where the future value of a cash flow is known, the same approach can be modified to calculate the present value based on its future value so that:

$$PV = \frac{FV}{(1 + r)^n}$$

Alternatively, this can be modified and expressed as a discount factor, calculated as:

$$PV = FV \times \frac{1}{(1+r)^n}$$

In the above example, if the future value after two years was known to be £1,210:

$$PV = £1,210 \times 1/1.21 \text{ so } PV = £1,210 \times 0.8264 = £1,000$$

In summary, the calculation tells us that the value today (the present value) of £1,210 received in two years' time (the future value) is £1,000 when a 10% discount factor is used. This approach is the basis for discounted cash flow analysis, illustrated in the second example below.

Net Present Value

Discounted cash flow (DCF) analysis recognises that cash received at some point in the future is less valuable than cash received today. This technique calculates the present value of a future cash flow by applying a discount factor to it to reflect the length of the time delay before the cash is actually received.

Net Present Value (NPV) is the difference between the present value of all the negative cash flows and the present value of all the positive cash flows during the life of the project. If the present value of cash inflows is greater than the present value of cash outflows, the project will generate a positive NPV. If the present value of benefits is less than the present value of costs, the project NPV will be negative.

When the project NPV is greater than zero, this means the financial return from the project is greater than the discount rate used to discount the cash flows. Conversely, if the project NPV is less than zero this means that the project has failed to achieve a rate of return equal to the discount rate.

Example

A cash investment of £10,000 has been made today in a capital asset that has a life of five years and has no commercial value at the end of that period. The project generates cash inflows of £2,600 in each of the five years. The calculation in screenshot 8.1 shows the project NPV using a discount factor of 8%.

Screenshot 8.1

	A	B	C	D	E	F	G	H
1		NPV	Present	1	2	3	4	5
2								
3	Project cash flows		-£10,000	£2,600	£2,600	£2,600	£2,600	£2,600
4								
5	8% discount factor			0.92593	0.85734	0.79383	0.73503	0.68058
6								
7	Present value	£381	-£10,000	£2,407	£2,229	£2,064	£1,911	£1,770
8								

In DCF analysis all cash flows are assumed to take place at the end of each year. If a cash flow is expected to occur early during a particular year, it is assumed that it will occur at the end of the previous year. This means that cash spent early in Year 1 is assumed to occur in Year 0 and the discount factor in this case is always 1, regardless of the discount rate used. The discount factors for the other years are calculated as:

$$\frac{1}{(1 + r)^n}$$

Where r is the rate of discount and n is the number of the year. So the year 2 discount factor in the example is calculated as:

$$\frac{1}{(1 + .08)^2} = 0.85734$$

The NPV has been calculated by adding together the present values of the project cash flows in each of the five years and the initial investment made at the start of the first year. The project shows a positive NPV of £381 and this means that that at a discount rate of 8% the project will create value for the investor. The positive NPV also indicates that the average rate of return over the life of the project is greater than the discount rate used for the NPV calculation. The decision rule for investments is that, subject to other considerations about specific project risks and any other non-financial considerations, a project is financially worthwhile if the NPV is positive or zero. It is not worthwhile if the project NPV is less than zero.

Internal rate of return (IRR)

The internal rate of return (IRR) method is an alternative approach to investment appraisal using DCF analysis. The project IRR is the average percentage rate of return over the life of the project. If the project IRR was to be used as the discount factor, the resulting NPV would be exactly zero. If a discount factor of less than the project IRR is used, the resulting project NPV will be positive. Conversely, if a discount factor greater than the IRR is applied, a negative NPV will result. This is illustrated in Figure 8.1.

Figure 8.1

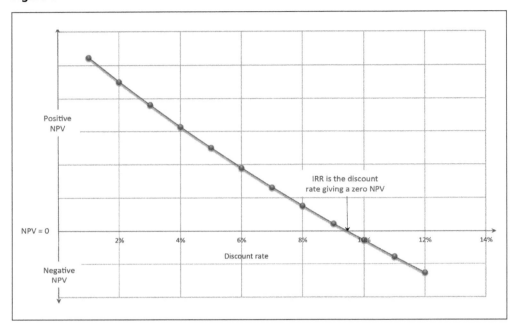

In the previous example, the project IRR is 9.435% and, when this rate is used as the discount factor for the DCF calculation, a zero NPV results.

Screenshot 8.2

	A	B	C	D	E	F	G	H
1		NPV	0	1	2	3	4	5
2								
3	Project cash flows		-£10,000	£2,600	£2,600	£2,600	£2,600	£2,600
4								
5	9.435% discount factor			0.91378	0.83500	0.76301	0.69723	0.63712
6								
7	Present value		£0	-£10,000	£2,376	£2,171	£1,984	£1,813	£1,657

Companies typically use IRR in conjunction with a hurdle rate of return that it aims to earn on its investment. If a project IRR were equal to or higher than the hurdle rate of return, it should be undertaken. A project IRR less than the hurdle rate of return would indicate that the project should be rejected.

Typically both NPV and IRR are calculated for a capital investment appraisal. Although some people find IRR a little easier to understand than the NPV concept, it is not advisable to rely solely on IRR for decision-making. IRR is a percentage measure and ignores the size of the investment. When choosing between two projects that are mutually exclusive, and only one of them can be chosen, the decision must always take into account the size of the investment. Compare the two projects in Screenshot 8.3 where the NPV has been calculated using a 15% discount factor.

Screenshot 8.3

	A	B	C
	Year	Project A	Project B
1			
2			
3	0	-£1,500	-£10,000
4	1	£400	£2,500
5	2	£550	£3,500
6	3	£750	£4,500
7	4	£800	£5,000
8			
9	NPV at 15%	£214	£638
10	IRR	21%	18%
11			

Although Project A shows a higher IRR than Project B, the size of the project means that Project B creates greater value, measured by the NPV. Caution is also needed when using IRR with non-conventional project cash flow patterns. Capital investment projects typically have negative cash flows in the first year followed by a number of years of positive cash flows. However, in some cases – say, for example, where there are significant costs at the end of a project in decommissioning a nuclear power plant – there may be negative project cash flows at the end of the project, as well as in the early years. In cases like this, where the sign changes from negative to positive then back to negative, it is possible that the project may have two or more different IRRs.

The Excel NPV function

The Excel NPV function calculates the net present value of an investment by using a discount rate and a series of future cash payments (negative values) and cash receipts (positive values). The form of the function is:

$$NPV(rate, value1, value2,...)$$

The NPV function has the following arguments:

- Rate is the discount factor to be used to calculate NPV.

- Value1, value2, ... must be equally spaced in time and, to interpret the order of cash flows, the payment and income values must be in the correct order. The values may also be entered in the function as a range of cells, as shown in the example below.

The NPV function treats each value as taking place at the end of each future period. If the initial cash flow takes place at the beginning of the first period, then this value must be excluded from the value arguments by the NPV function and added to the NPV result. If there are zero values in any of the values in the function range, it is important to enter a zero rather than leaving the cell empty, as this will produce an incorrect NPV result.

Example

A cash investment of £5,000 has been made at the start of year 1 in an asset that has a life of three years and has no commercial value at the end of that period. The project generates cash inflows of £2,000 in each of the three years. The calculation below shows the project NPV using a discount factor of 10%.

Screenshot 8.4

	A	B	C	D	E	F
1		NPV	0	1	2	3
2						
3	Project cash flows	-£26	-£5,000	£2,000	£2,000	£2,000
4						
5						

The NPV function is used as shown below:

Screenshot 8.5

	A	B	C	D	E	F
1		NPV	0	1	2	3
2						
3	Project cash flows	=NPV(0.1,D3:F3)+C3	-5000	2000	2000	2000
4						
5						

The 10% discount factor is entered as a decimal. The NPV function is applied to the values for years 1 to 3 and the value calculated by the NPV function is added to the value in cell C3 that represents the initial cash flow at the beginning of period 1, shown as period 0.

The Excel IRR function

The IRR function calculates the internal rate of return for a series of cash flows represented by the numbers in values, which must occur at regular intervals, such as monthly or annually. The form of the function is:

$$IRR(values,guess)$$

The IRR function has the following arguments:

- Values is an array or a reference to cells that contain numbers for which the internal rate of return is to be calculated. Values must contain at least one positive and one negative value to calculate IRR.

- IRR uses the order of values to interpret the order of cash flows. Make sure the payment and income values are in the correct sequence.

- If an array or reference argument contains text, logical values or empty cells, those values are ignored.

- Guess is a guess of the IRR result. It is rarely necessary to enter a guess and if it is omitted, it is assumed to be 0.1 (in other words, 10%). If IRR produces the #NUM! error, or if the result appears incorrect, it might be worth entering a value for 'guess' and recalculating IRR.

Using the previous example:

Screenshot 8.6

	A	B	C	D	E	F
1		IRR	0	1	2	3
2						
3	Project cash flows	9.7%	-£5,000	£2,000	£2,000	£2,000
4						
5						

The IRR function is used in the above example as shown in Screenshot 8.7.

Screenshot 8.7

	A	B	C	D	E	F
1		IRR	0	1	2	3
2						
3	Project cash flows	=IRR(C3:F3)	-5000	2000	2000	2000
4						
5						

Relevant costs and benefits for investment decisions

The relevant costs and benefits on which investment decisions should be made are the incremental cash flows that arise directly as a result of undertaking the investment. The implications of this are:

- Using DCF analysis, the investment decision is based entirely on cash flows, so non-cash items – like depreciation, amortisation and impairment write-offs or provisions – should be ignored.

- Relevant costs are future cash flows – costs that have already been incurred are not relevant to making a decision about a prospective investment. For example, any costs incurred on a previously abandoned project that is under consideration for reinstatement and completion should be ignored. These sunk costs are irretrievable, whether or not the investment is made.

- Relevant costs arise entirely as a result of the investment decision. If the costs were to be incurred regardless of the decision they are not relevant.

- If the investment project uses existing resources that have an alternative use, the value of the benefit forgone by using this resource must be included as a relevant cost. For example, if a project uses company-owned land that might otherwise have been leased on the open market, the opportunity cost is the loss of rent that might otherwise have been received.

- When the benefits from an investment are in the form of profit from selling products or services, it is important that the impact of changes to working capital and operating cash flow are accurately reflected. Chapter 6 described how changes in sales revenue usually cause changes in the level of net working capital, which had the effect of increasing or reducing operating cash flow. This is illustrated in the Investment Decision Model.

- When an investment results in higher profits, there will also be higher taxation and the resulting tax cash flows should be included as relevant costs. The timing and size of tax cash flows may also be influenced by the relevant tax rules on the calculation of capital allowances on plant and equipment. It may be necessary to take expert advice on how to base assumptions about the amount and timing of tax cash flows.

Interest and dividends represent payments to the providers of the company's capital. Both are ignored for the purposes of DCF analysis because the cost of funding is implicitly reflected in the calculation by applying a discount factor to the cash flows.

Which discount rate to use

The aim of any investment appraisal tool is to identify an investment opportunity that will create the greatest value for shareholders. Value is created when the return generated by an investment is greater than the cost of financing it, so the discount rate might be related to the cost of borrowed funds, or to the overall cost of the company's capital structure – comprising share capital and debt capital. This is commonly calculated as weighted average cost of capital (WACC) and is discussed further in Chapter 10. Were the cost of finance to be used as the discount factor, a positive NPV would indicate that the return from the investment would at least cover the cost of financing it. However, as companies focus on creating value for shareholders in excess of the cost of finance, it is common for companies to establish a hurdle rate that will provide a margin in excess of the WACC. For example, if a company's WACC was 11%, a discount factor of 15% might be used for investment appraisal decisions – either as a discount factor to calculate NPV, or as a target rate for IRR.

The return on an investment must also be considered in the context of the risk involved in the investment. Where an investment involves a greater than average level of risk by, for example, investing in a new country, there may be a case for adding an additional risk premium to the hurdle rate.

DCF and inflation

When a company makes a long-term investment there is always the possibility that future revenues and costs will be affected by inflation. In practice, inflation is usually ignored in investment analysis because it is usually the case that:

- There is not expected to be any significant inflation in prices and costs, or
- it is impossible to predict what the effect of inflation will be, or
- all investment cash flows, both benefits and costs, would be subject to a similar rate of inflation.

Where inflation might be a significant factor, for example, making an investment in a region subject to high levels of inflation, inflationary risks should be taken in to account – always assuming that reasonable estimates of the future rate of inflation can be made. In this case the cash flows in each year should be increased by the rate of inflation for the full year. An inflated future cash flow for year n, where i is the annual rate of inflation, can be calculated as:

$$Cash\ flow\ at\ current\ price\ \times (1 + i)^n$$

The discount factor used for DCF analysis is usually related to the company's cost of capital, which is itself based on market rates for debt and equity finance. Market returns and yields implicitly reflect the markets' own expectations of future inflation rates so, when the discount factor has been based on company cost of capital, it can be used to discount the inflated cash flows.

DCF investment analysis – practical methodology

In projects where the free cash flows are expected to vary over their whole life, for example, crude oil production facilities in which output increases to a peak and then declines over the life of the oilfield, it may be necessary to calculate the free cash flow for each year of the project. Many other types of project lend themselves to a simpler approach – for example, a chemical processing plant may have a life of 25 years or more and, although it is important to consider all of the cash flows over this lifetime, it is unnecessary to make 25 or more separate present value calculations.

It usually takes some time to bring something like a processing plant to full productive capacity and to develop the market for its products. Typically, project revenues then continue to grow for a number of years before stabilising at a level that may be maintained for the productive life of the plant. In this situation, a practical two-stage approach to the DCF investment analysis (illustrated in the Investment Decision Model) can be adopted:

- **First stage**: A detailed forecast of benefits and costs is made for each of the years during which the investment is developing and growing. This is the so-called discrete period, or competitive advantage period, which often works out to be five years.

- **Second stage**: An estimate is made of the present value of all of the future cash flows for the remainder of the life of the investment project, comprising the revenues and costs for the remaining years and the disposal value of any equipment and working capital at the end of this period. This is referred to as the terminal, or residual, value and is included as a cash flow in the final year of the discrete period. The terminal value is discounted at the same discount rate as the other cash flows in the final year of the discrete period.

Calculating terminal value

There are a number of approaches to estimating the terminal value of an investment. For an investment with a relatively short life, for example a piece of equipment that might be replaced with a more up to date asset after five years, the terminal value might be included on the basis of the disposal value of the equipment. When cash flows are expected to continue for a number of years following the end of the discrete period, an annuity approach can be used to estimate terminal value.

An annuity is a constant cash flow for a given number of future time periods. Its present value (*PV*) could be calculated by applying the DCF approach to each of the periods, as described above, but the formula below can be used to calculate the present value in one step:

$$PV = \frac{A}{r} \times \left[1 - \frac{1}{(1 + r)^n} \right]$$

Where:

A = the constant cash flow

r = the discount rate, as a decimal

n = the number of periods

Example

Investment project cash flows are expected to continue at a constant rate of £250,000 per year for ten years following the end of the discrete period. The investment assets have no value at the end of the ten years. A discount rate of 12% is being used for the DCF analysis.

$$PV = \frac{£250,000}{0.12} \times \left[1 - \frac{1}{(1.12)^{10}} \right] = £2,083,333 \times 0.678027 = £1,412,556$$

Alternatively, the Excel PV function may be used to calculate the present value of an annuity.

The Excel PV function

PV is an Excel financial function that calculates the present value of an investment with a constant cash flow and discount rate. The basic form of the function is:

$$PV(rate, nper, pmt)$$

The arguments in the function are:

- rate: this is the same discount rate as is being used in the discounted cash flow analysis
- nper: is the number of periods for which the annuity calculation is required
- pmt: is the constant cash flow for each year of the annuity

Annuity growth method

The annuity growth method allows for an increase in the cash flows during the annuity period. The calculation is based on the basic form of the annuity calculation with the addition of an argument for the growth rate, represented below as 'g'.

$$PV = \frac{A}{r - g} \times \left[1 - \left(\frac{1 + g}{1 + r}\right)^n\right]$$

A perpetuity is a constant annual cash flow that continues forever in to the future. The present value of a perpetuity is calculated as:

$$PV = \frac{A}{r}$$

Where:

A = the constant cash flow

r = the discount rate, as a decimal

When using discount factors in excess of 10%, the value of an annuity approaches that of a perpetuity after around 20 years and, using this simpler method, provides a satisfactory estimate of the terminal value.

The Investment Decision Model workbook

The workbook comprises two worksheets: an input sheet and a calculation sheet for the DCF analysis. The NPV and IRR for the investment are both displayed on the input sheet so that the impact of any changes in the assumptions can be seen as soon as they have been applied.

There are many different kinds of investment applications to which DCF analysis can be applied. (Business valuation is one of these applications and this is discussed separately in Chapter 10.) To illustrate, as far as is possible, the principles discussed above, the model has been set up to deal with a common type of decision involving a proposed investment in a new manufacturing facility.

Input worksheet for the Investment Decision Model

Screenshot 8.8

	A	B	C	D	E	F	G
1	INVESTMENT DECISION ASSUMPTIONS						
2	£000's omitted	0	1	2	3	4	5
3	Initial investment	£100,000					
4	Sales revenue		£45,000	£70,000	£100,000	£120,000	£135,000
5	Cost of goods sold % of revenue		45%	45%	45%	45%	45%
6	Operating costs % of revenue		30%	30%	30%	30%	30%
7	Capital allowance for tax purposes		£3,000	£3,000	£3,000	£3,000	£3,000
8	Tax % of profit		15%	15%	15%	15%	15%
9	Inventory days		90	90	90	90	90
10	Receivables days		60	60	60	60	60
11	Payables days		40	40	40	40	40
12	Plant and equipment replacement		£0	£2,000	£3,000	£5,000	£5,000
13	Full life of project - years	20					
14	End of life value of assets	£60,000					
15	Discount rate	15.0%					
16							
17	Project NPV	£1,562					
18	Project IRR	15.4%					

This illustration represents a new manufacturing facility with a life of 20 years and an initial investment of £100m, made at the commencement of the first year. The model uses a discrete period of five years during which the plant becomes fully operational and the sales revenue growth represents the development of the full market potential for its products. It is assumed that sales revenues will be maintained after year 5 and inflation has been ignored on the assumption that it is likely to remain at benign levels and apply equally to both benefits and costs.

Sales revenue assumptions have been entered directly, but for years 2 to 5 they could also have been expressed as a percentage growth over the previous year.

The cost of goods sold assumption is expressed as a percentage of sales revenue as these costs tend to be largely variable. Other operating costs have also been entered as a percentage of sales revenue though, in practice, there is usually a fixed component to these costs. If necessary, the input assumptions can be changed to reflect this. Other operating costs exclude non-cash charges like depreciation, amortisation or asset impairment charges.

An annual capital allowance is entered for the purposes of calculating the taxable profit on which to base the tax payment. The percentage tax rate is applied to this profit.

The working capital calculations are based on assumptions for inventory days, receivables days and creditor days. Chapter 3 described how Days' Sales Outstanding (DSO) could be calculated as:

$$DSO = \frac{Trade\ debtors}{Sales\ revenue} \times 365$$

When DSO and sales revenue are known, trade debtors can be calculated as:

$$Trade\ debtors = \frac{DSO}{365} \times Sales\ revenue$$

A similar approach can be used to calculate inventory and payables using cost of sales rather than sales revenue in these formulae.

Plant and equipment replacement represents additional cash payments made during the life of the project to maintain the productive capacity of the plant.

The end of life value of the assets should include the sale or scrap value of the productive assets, plus the end of life value of the working capital.

The discount factor is that which will be used in the DCF analysis.

The DCF analysis

Screenshot 8.9

	A	B	C	D	E	F	G
1	DISCOUNTED CASH FLOW ANALYSIS						
2	£000's omitted	0	1	2	3	4	5
3	Initial investment	£(100,000)					
4	Sales revenue		£45,000	£70,000	£100,000	£120,000	£135,000
5	Cost of goods sold		£(20,250)	£(31,500)	£(45,000)	£(54,000)	£(60,750)
6	Operating costs		£(13,500)	£(21,000)	£(30,000)	£(36,000)	£(40,500)
7	Tax paid			£(1,238)	£(2,175)	£(3,300)	£(4,050)
8	Operating cash flow		£11,250	£16,263	£22,825	£26,700	£29,700
9							
10	Inventory		£4,993	£7,767	£11,096	£13,315	£14,979
11	Receivables		£7,397	£11,507	£16,438	£19,726	£22,192
12	Payables		£(2,219)	£(3,452)	£(4,932)	£(5,918)	£(6,658)
13	Net working capital		£10,171	£15,822	£22,602	£27,123	£30,513
14	Change in net working capital		£(10,171)	£(5,651)	£(6,780)	£(4,521)	£(3,390)
15							
16	Plant and equipment replacement		£0	£(2,000)	£(3,000)	£(5,000)	£(5,000)
17							
18	Maintainable post-tax operating cash flow						£21,138
19	Annuity value of post tax operating cash flow						£123,602
20	Present value of end of life value of assets						£7,374
21	Terminal value						£130,976
22							
23	NET CASH FLOWS	£(100,000)	£1,079	£8,612	£13,045	£17,179	£152,286
24							
25	Project NPV	£1,562					
26	Project IRR	15.4%					

INPUT | DCF ANALYSIS | +

The formulae used to generate the cash flows in periods 0 and 1 are shown in Screenshot 8.10.

Screenshot 8.10

	A	B	C
1	**DISCOUNTED CASH FLOW ANALYSIS**		
2	£000's omitted	0	1
3	Initial investment	=-INPUT!B3	
4	Sales revenue		=INPUT!C4
5	Cost of goods sold		=-ROUND(INPUT!C4*INPUT!C5,0)
6	Operating costs		=-ROUND(INPUT!C4*INPUT!C6,0)
7	Tax paid		
8	**Operating cash flow**		=SUM(C4:C7)
9			
10	Inventory		=ROUND(INPUT!C4*INPUT!C5*INPUT!C9/365,0)
11	Receivables		=ROUND(INPUT!C4*INPUT!C10/365,0)
12	Payables		=-ROUND(INPUT!C4*INPUT!C5*INPUT!C11/365,0)
13	Net working capital		=SUM(C10:C12)
14	**Change in net working capital**		=-C13
15			
16	**Plant and equipment replacement**		=-INPUT!C12

The initial investment is taken from the Input sheet and expressed as a negative cash flow in cell B3. Sales revenue is also taken from the Input sheet and the percentage assumptions from the Input sheet are used to calculate the cost of goods sold and operating costs – both expressed as negative cash flows. The DCF analysis assumes that tax is paid one year after the year in which the profit is actually made, so there is no tax payment in year 1.

Working capital is calculated based on the assumptions for inventory days, receivables days and payables days, as described above. Note that the payables component is expressed as a negative figure to calculate net working capital. An increase in net working capital will reduce cash flow and, in year 1, the impact of this is equal to an increase from zero working capital to the level at the end of year 1. The plant and equipment replacement costs are taken from the Input sheet and expressed as a negative cash flow.

The formulae used to generate the recurring investment cash flows in years 2 to 5 of the discrete period are the same, and are shown in Screenshot 8.11 for year 2.

Screenshot 8.11

	A	D
1	DISCOUNTED CASH FLOW ANALYSIS	
2	£000's omitted	2
3	Initial investment	
4	Sales revenue	=INPUT!D4
5	Cost of goods sold	=-ROUND(INPUT!D4*INPUT!D5,0)
6	Operating costs	=-ROUND(INPUT!D4*INPUT!D6,0)
7	Tax paid	=-(C4+C5+C6-INPUT!C7)*INPUT!C8
8	**Operating cash flow**	=SUM(D4:D7)
9		
10	Inventory	=ROUND(INPUT!D4*INPUT!D5*INPUT!D9/365,0)
11	Receivables	=ROUND(INPUT!D4*INPUT!D10/365,0)
12	Payables	=-ROUND(INPUT!D4*INPUT!D5*INPUT!D11/365,0)
13	Net working capital	=SUM(D10:D12)
14	**Change in net working capital**	=C13-D13
15		
16	**Plant and equipment replacement**	=-INPUT!D12
17		

Sales revenue, the cost of goods sold and operating costs are calculated on the same basis as year 1. The tax paid in year 2 is based on year 1 profit, after applying the capital allowance assumption from the Input sheet. If the project makes a tax loss in the first year, the tax will be expressed as a positive cash flow in year 2 – this implicitly assumes that the tax loss on the investment project can be applied as group relief on the profit from the rest of the business. Some practitioners might argue that this kind of external cash flow should not be included in an appraisal of a specific project, but in any event a tax loss in the early years of a project can be relieved against profits in the later years. So, in the worst case this treatment will result only in the early recognition of the tax loss benefit. A more complex set of formulae could no doubt be used to model this more accurately if it was material to the outcome of the project.

Working capital is calculated in the same manner as year 1, but the impact on cash flow reflects the change in the level of working capital from year 1 to year 2.

The formulae used to calculate the terminal value are shown in Screenshot 8.12.

Screenshot 8.12

	A	G
1	DISCOUNTED CASH FLOW ANALYSIS	
2	£000's omitted	5
17		
18	Maintainable post-tax operating cash flow	=ROUND((SUM(G4:G6)-INPUT!G7)*(1-INPUT!G8),0)-INPUT!G12
19	Annuity value of post tax operating cash flow	=ROUND(G18/INPUT!B15*(1-1/(1+INPUT!B15)^(INPUT!B13-5)),0)
20	Present value of end of life value of assets	=ROUND(INPUT!B14*1/(1+INPUT!B15)^(INPUT!B13-5),0)
21	Terminal value	=G19+G20
22		

Maintainable annual post-tax operating cash flow is based on the cash flows for the final year of the discrete period. Profit is calculated after deducting the tax that would be paid on that final year profit, rather than on the prior year profit. The plant and equipment replacement for the final year of the discrete period is deducted from this after-tax profit. Since it is assumed that revenues will remain stable during the residual period of the project, it is further assumed that there would be no change in working capital levels during the same period.

The annuity value of the maintainable annual post-tax operating cash flow is calculated in the manner described above – the period for the annuity is based on the full life of the project minus the five-year discrete period. In the example, the annuity is based on a 15-year (20 years total minus five years discrete period) residual period.

The present value of the end-of-life value of the assets is based on the assumption in the Input sheet. This assumption should include the estimated disposal value of the physical assets and the cash benefit of the elimination of the working capital when trading ceases. The present value is calculated by discounting the total asset value by the discount factor applicable at the end of the 15th year of the residual period. The total terminal value of the investment project is calculated by adding the annuity value of the maintainable cash flows to the present value of the assets.

It was explained in the section above that, in general, when the project IRR is used as a discount factor, the project NPV will then be exactly zero. In this application the annuity value used as the terminal value of the project is calculated using the discount factor, thus creating a circular function in which the IRR would itself be modified were it to be used to determine the residual value. If the terminal value were to be converted to a fixed numerical value, then using the IRR as a discount factor would produce a zero NPV.

The net cash flows in row 23 of the DCF Analysis are calculated by adding together the operating cash flows, the cash flow effect of changes in net working capital, plant and equipment replacement and the terminal value. The project NPB and IRR are calculated using the Excel functions described above. Note how the NPV function has been applied to the net cash flows for years 1 to 5 and then added to the initial investment. The formulae for the NPV and IRR functions are as shown in Screenshot 8.13.

Screenshot 8.13

	A	B
1	DISCOUNTED CASH FLOW ANALYSIS	
2	£000's omitted	0
23	NET CASH FLOWS	=B3
24		
25	Project NPV	=NPV(INPUT!B15,'DCF ANALYSIS (2)'!C23:G23)+'DCF ANALYSIS (2)'!B23
26	Project IRR	=IRR(B23:G23)
27		

The NPV and the IRR are duplicated on the Input sheet and this makes the effect of any changes to the assumptions immediately visible. The sensitivity of the investment project to various kinds of risks can thus be easily tested.

The illustration used for the Investment Decision Model is a common, if slightly complicated, example of the kind of decision to which the DCF approach lends itself. In other cases, for example the prospective investment in a single machine, the decision parameters may be somewhat less complex and the illustrative model may be adapted accordingly.

The acquisition of another business is one of the most common forms of capital investment requiring an appraisal in the form of a business valuation. The methodology used by investment analysts and corporate finance professionals is explained and illustrated in Chapter 10.

Chapter 9

Model 6: Financial Statement Forecasting

From the perspective of someone who has worked in business for more than 30 years, the most profound change over that period has been the rate of change itself. In today's globally competitive world, we face unprecedented levels of risk and uncertainty. In an era when the price of crude oil can collapse by 70% over the course of a few months, it is vital to use forecasting models that can facilitate the kind of business analysis that helps us to understand the likely impact of these types of risk events on organisational performance – and results.

The Financial Statement Forecasting Model

- **Users:** A financial analyst, chief financial officer or financial manager would typically use this financial model to test the sensitivity of key financial measures to the various types of risk events that the business might encounter.

- **Purpose:** The model uses as few key driver inputs as necessary to generate a set of financial statement forecasts from which key financial measures, like Return on Net Assets and profit margin, for example, can be calculated.

- **Outputs:** The output is in the form of a set of conventional financial statements and an executive summary of key measures for the forecasting period.

- **Inputs:** There is one Excel INPUT worksheet for the 25 or so key driver assumptions that are used to generate a full set of financial statements.

- **Calculations:** The calculations for the components of the financial statements are incorporated into the outputs of the financial statements themselves.

- **Design:** Key driver assumptions are entered into the INPUT sheet. Calculation and output is combined in the four output sheets for the financial statements and the executive summary.

Topic refresher – the impact of risk on financial performance

Much of the decision making in business involves some element of risk or uncertainty. Decisions are based on what the decision-maker thinks will happen, but there is invariably some possibility that the actual outcome will be different, perhaps better or possibly worse than expected.

Uncertainty arises from a lack of information about what is likely to happen in the future, increasing the likelihood that forecasts for sales revenues and costs, for example, will be inaccurate. Although access to additional high-quality information may, to some extent, reduce uncertainty, by its very nature it is unlikely that it can be completely eliminated. Sales forecasts for well-established products may be based on statistical analyses of historical sales and adjusted for the effects of expected volume growth and price changes – but even in these cases uncertainty around changes in market demographics and consumer tastes will remain. When forecasting sales of new products, without historical data on the pattern and trend of past sales, the uncertainty will be even greater.

Risk is present when the future outcome from a decision could be one of several different possibilities – but it may sometimes be possible to determine with reasonable accuracy the probability of each possible outcome and use statistical analysis to form a view of the result. There is uncertainty or risk in most aspects of business, so decision makers must always consider the potential effect of risk on the expected incremental costs and benefits. A number of techniques are commonly used.

Expected values

Expected values can be used to analyse information where risk can be assessed in terms of probabilities of different outcomes. When probabilities are assigned to each of the different outcomes, the result of the decision can be quantified as the expected value or weighted average of these outcomes.

$$Expected\ value\ (EV)\ =\ weighted\ average\ of\ possible\ outcomes$$

The weighted average value is calculated by applying the probability of each possible outcome to the value of each outcome:

$$EV\ =\ \Sigma px$$

Where p represents the probability of each outcome and x represents the value of each outcome, resulting in a weighted average value.

Example

A firm must select one of three projects for investment; the three projects are mutually exclusive and only one of them may be selected. The projects do not involve any initial capital expenditures. The expected annual cash flows generated by each of the projects will depend on the state of the market. The table below shows estimates of annual cash flows for each project.

State of market:	Falling	Static	Rising
Probability	0.2	0.3	0.5
	000's	000's	000's
Project 1	£100	£200	£900
Project 2	£0	£500	£600
Project 3	£180	£190	£200

The pay-off matrix above shows all of the possible outcomes from different decisions or strategies under different market conditions. The data from the matrix can be used to calculate the expected value (EV) of the annual cash flows, shown in the table below.

Market	Probability	Project 1		Project 2		Project 3	
		Profit	EV	Profit	EV	Profit	EV
		000's	000's	000's	000's	000's	000's
Falling	0.2	£100	£20	£0	£0	£180	£36
Static	0.3	£200	£60	£500	£150	£190	£57
Rising	0.5	£900	£450	£600	£300	£200	£100
			£530		£450		£193

According to the EV calculation above, Project 1 would be selected on the basis that it delivered the highest expected value for annual cash flow. This approach to managing risk has the advantage of taking into account all of the possible outcomes that have been identified and the probability that each will occur. It also recognises the risk in making decisions based on the probabilities of each of the possible outcomes, expressing the risk in a single figure – which makes it easy to compare different options and reach a decision.

In practice it tends to be difficult to estimate the probabilities of the various possible outcomes and if the probabilities are unreliable, expected values will also inevitably be unreliable, and of little use. The weighted average approach also means that the EV is unlikely to be an actual outcome that might occur, so unless the same decision is to be duplicated many times, the EV is unlikely to be ever achieved.

Simulation modelling

In real-life business decision making, there are often many different variables, each with different probable outcomes, and the relationship between these variables may be complex. In this type of situation, much more information is required about risk and the range of possible outcomes, rather than just the expected value of the most likely outcome. In these kinds of applications, a more sophisticated simulation model might be needed to deal with the level of complexity involved.

Monte Carlo simulation modelling

Monte Carlo simulation modelling may be used in the context of more complicated probability-based decision making – this type of model typically employs a large number of interrelated variables and estimated probabilities for each of their different possible values. These probabilities are then used to assign a range of random numbers to each variable – the allocation of these random numbers reflecting the probability distribution. The model can then be used to calculate the value of the outcome or result for a given set of values for each variable, determined by the generation of random numbers for each variable. The process is repeated to generate a large number of different iterations based on different sets of random numbers generated by Excel – or other more specialised software applications. Further analysis can be used to produce a probability distribution of the data generated that can then produce a further statistical analysis of the risk in a given situation.

Simulation of this kind provides more information about the possible outcomes and their relative probabilities, and makes it possible to statistically analyse the risk involved in a business decision, making it useful for complex problems. But it is not a technique for decision-making. It is only a method for generating more information about the risks and probabilities of different possible outcomes.

Scenario analysis

Scenario analysis provides a range of alternative future events based on the impact that various risk events may have on them. The approach does not attempt to arrive at one definitive view, but offers a number of possible scenarios – typically a *best case, worst case* and a *most likely case* is produced. Excel's Scenario Manager tool may be useful in this context.

Sensitivity analysis

Sensitivity, or *what-if* analysis, is an approach to modelling risk and uncertainty that tests the effect on the expected outcome of changes in the values of key variables, or key factors. For example, in planning and forecasting, the effect on planned profit might be tested for changes in sales volume or product prices during the forecast period. When these types of estimates are uncertain, what-if analysis is useful for assessing what might happen if the estimates prove to be wrong. For example, if management consider that their estimates of sales volumes might be inaccurate by up to 20%, sensitivity analysis can be used to assess what the result would be if sales volume were 20% less than estimated.

Forecasting financial statements for sensitivity analysis

There are a number of situations in which it is necessary to prepare detailed forecasts for financial statements to assess the financial performance and strength of an organisation. This is done by providing the basis for calculating the kind of financial indicators described in Chapter 3, for example, when forecasting a company's projected results for the financial year in order to compare to an earlier plan or budget for the same period. Projected financial statements are also a fundamental component of business plan presentations to potential investors who will want to test the underlying drivers of the key financial performance measures.

Conventional approach to forecasting financial statements

The conventional approach to forecasting financial statements focuses on the outputs from the forecast process and typically uses the framework of the organisation's financial accounting system. This approach usually employs a large Excel spreadsheet that may run to hundreds of lines. This focus on detailed output makes the forecast unwieldy and difficult to change if the impact of various kinds of risk events on the firm's results are to be tested. In one well-known global charge card company, the financial statement forecast used more than 200 lines and took eight weeks to prepare for the whole group, making the forecasts inflexible and all but impossible to use for *what-if* sensitivity analysis.

Key business drivers

The charge card company identified the key business drivers that affected 80% of their numbers – these key drivers represented just 15 lines of the old style forecast. Customer revenue, for example, was previously forecast in detail using more than 30 lines, but in reality it was dependent on just two key input drivers: the number of charge cards in issue at any time, and the average spend on each card. By focusing on the inputs to the forecast and using a minimum number of key business drivers, their forecasting process was simplified and accelerated, making it much more powerful as a tool for helping to assess and manage the impact of potential risk events and business uncertainties.

Figure 9.1

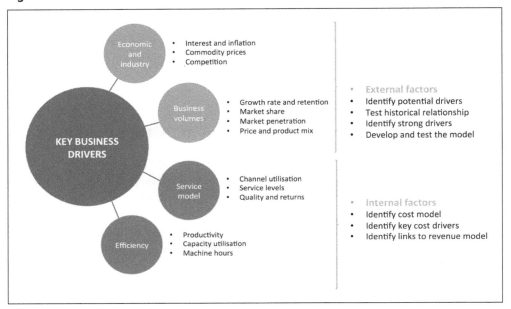

Both external and internal drivers influence business performance. In some industries, like oil, gas and petrochemicals, commodity prices and dollar exchange rates are key factors. For many other firms, sales volumes may be dependent on factors like market growth potential, customer retention rates and market penetration. Internal drivers may include capacity utilisation levels and production reject levels, in addition to production cost and working capital drivers.

A business will usually identify a combination of internal and external factors that may be relevant key business drivers. Some external factors may be fairly obvious; for example, the market price of crude oil in the oil and gas sector. Less obvious drivers may be identified using analysis of historical financial data or using problem-solving tools like brainstorming. Internal drivers may be easier to identify based on an understanding of the firm's markets, supply chain and cost structure.

Once a set of likely drivers has been identified, their historical relationship to financial performance can be tested using, for example, regression and correlation methods. The strongest drivers for use in producing forecasts are thus identified.

The Financial Statement Forecasting Model workbook

The workbook comprises five worksheets: an input sheet, combined calculation and output sheets for the executive summary, income statement, balance sheet and cash flow statement.

The illustration represents the Omicron Design Company Limited. The company's financial statements are shown below and provide the opening balances included in the input assumptions below.

OMICRON DESIGN COMPANY LIMITED

Statement of comprehensive income for year ending 31st December

£000's omitted	2016	2015
Sales	143,000	132,000
Cost of sales	(94,380)	(85,800)
Gross profit	48,620	46,200
Administrative expenses	(31,000)	(28,000)
Depreciation	(4,000)	(3,600)
Operating profit	**13,620**	**14,600**
Finance costs	(950)	(1,050)
Profit before tax	12,670	13,550
Taxation	(2,787)	(2,981)
Profit for the year	**9,883**	**10,569**
Other comprehensive income		
Total comprehensive income for the year	**9,883**	**10,569**

OMICRON DESIGN COMPANY LIMITED

Statement of changes in shareholders' equity

£000's omitted	Share capital	Revaluation reserve	Retained earnings	Total
Balance at 31st December 2014	10,000	1,650	35,405	47,055
Dividend payments			(5,000)	(5,000)
Profit for the year			10,569	10,569
Balance at 31st December 2015	10,000	1,650	40,974	52,624
Dividend payments			(5,000)	(5,000)
Profit for the year			9,883	9,883
Balance at 31st December 2016	**10,000**	**1,650**	**45,857**	**57,507**

OMICRON DESIGN COMPANY LIMITED

Statement of financial position as at 31st December

£000's omitted	2016	2015
Non-current assets		
Property, plant and equipment	35,300	35,800
	35,300	35,800
Current assets		
Inventories	8,619	6,998
Trade receivables	29,384	25,315
Cash and cash equivalents	3,470	5,806
	41,473	38,119
Current liabilities		
Trade and other payables	(5,516)	(4,665)

Borrowings	(3,000)	(3,000)
Current tax liability	(400)	(250)
	(8,916)	(7,915)
Net current assets	**32,557**	**30,204**

Non-current liabilities

Borrowings	(10,000)	(13,000)
Deferred tax liabilities	(250)	(230)
Provisions	(100)	(150)
Net assets	**57,507**	**52,624**
Share capital	10,000	10,000
Reserves	1,650	1,650
Retained earnings	45,857	40,974
Shareholders' equity	**57,507**	**52,624**

Property, plant and equipment

£000's omitted	Land and buildings	Plant and equipment	Fixtures and fittings	Total
Cost				
Balance at 1st January 2015	27,500	33,300	4,700	65,500
Additions		3,500		3,500
Disposals				
Balance 31st December 2015	**27,500**	**36,800**	**4,700**	**69,000**
Balance 1st January 2016	27,500	36,800	4,700	69,000
Additions		3,500		3,500

Disposals			
Balance 31st December 2016	**27,500**	**40,300**	**4,700**	**72,500**

Accumulated depreciation

Balance at 1st January 2015	450	26,750	2,400	29,600
Depreciation for the year	150	3,000	450	3,600
Disposals				
Balance 31st December 2015	**600**	**29,750**	**2,850**	**33,200**
Balance 1st January 2016	600	29,750	2,850	33,200
Depreciation for the year	150	3,400	450	4,000
Disposals				
Balance 31st December 2016	**750**	**33,150**	**3,300**	**37,200**

Carrying amounts

At 31st December 2015	**26,900**	**7,050**	**1,850**	**35,800**
At 31st December 2016	**26,750**	**7,150**	**1,400**	**35,300**

OMICRON DESIGN COMPANY LIMITED

Statement of cash flows for year ending 31st December

£000's omitted	2015	2014
Operating profit	13,620	14,600
Depreciation	4,000	3,600
Interest paid	(950)	(1,050)
Tax paid	(2,637)	(2,931)
	14,033	14,219
(Increase)/decrease in inventory	(1,621)	(423)
(Increase)/decrease in receivables	(4,069)	(3,945)

(Decrease)/increase in trade and other payables	851	720
(Decrease)/increase in provisions	(30)	100
Net cash generated from operating activities	**9,164**	**10,671**
Purchase of plant and equipment	(3,500)	(3,500)
Net cash used in investing activities	**(3,500)**	**(3,500)**
Repayment of borrowings	(3,000)	(3,000)
Dividend payments	(5,000)	(5,000)
Net cash used in financing activities	**(8,000)**	**(8,000)**
Net change in cash and cash equivalents	**(2,336)**	**(829)**
Cash and cash equivalents at start of the year	5,806	6,635
Cash and cash equivalents at end of the year	**3,470**	**5,806**

Input sheet for the Financial Statement Forecasting Model

Screenshot 9.1

	A	B	C	D	E	F
1	**FINANCIAL STATEMENT ASSUMPTIONS**	assumptions in £000's unless stated otherwise				
2	Entity name	Omicron Design Company Limited				
3	Period ending date	31st December				
4	Periods	2016	2017	2018	2019	
5	**Income statement**					
6	Sales revenue		144,000	146,000	147,000	
7	Cost of goods sold - % of revenue		44.0%	43.3%	43.0%	
8	Direct overhead costs		32,000	33,000	34,000	
9	Indirect overhead costs		32,000	33,000	34,000	
10	Effective tax rate on profit		22.0%	22.0%	22.0%	
11	**Non-current assets**					
12	Opening balance at cost	72,500				
13	Additions		6,000	6,000	6,000	
14	Disposals at cost		2,500			
15	Proceeds from disposals		750			
16	Depreciation opening balance	37,200				
17	Depreciation for the year		4,000	4,500	5,000	
18	Accumulated depreciation on disposals		2,000			
19	**Working capital**		Working capital cycle days			
20	Inventory	8,619	52	45	50	
21	Receivables	29,384	71	70	65	
22	Trade payables	5,516	31	30	30	
23	**Borrowing**					
24	Opening balance	13,000				
25	New borrowing					
26	Repayment		2,000	2,000	2,000	2,000
27	Interest paid		700	600	500	

Screenshot 9.2

	A	B	C	D	E	F
28	**Shareholders equity**					
29	Share capital	10,000				
30	Reserves	1,650				
31	Retained earnings	45,857				
32	Dividend payments		5,000	5,000	5,000	
33	**Other liabilities**					
34	Opening tax creditor	400				
35	Current tax creditor % of tax payable		22.0%	22.0%	22.0%	
36	Deferred tax and other provisions	350	360	370	350	
37						
38						
39						
40						

The input assumptions in columns B, C, D and E above are used to generate the financial statements for the forecast period 2017 to 2019. There is an additional assumption in cell F26 for the amount of borrowing to be repaid in the year following the end of the forecast period. This is used for the balance sheet classification (if necessary) as current liabilities, of borrowings to be repaid within 12 months of the end of the final forecast period.

Simplicity is one of the key attributes of an effective financial model, and this often means resisting the temptation to make the model more complex than necessary. The input assumptions are based on typical key business drivers and the relationship between them, and allows changes in these drivers to be properly reflected in the financial performance and financial position presented in the financial statements.

Income statement forecast

The input assumptions in columns C, D and E are used to produce a standard statement of comprehensive income. A published statement of comprehensive income might typically also show amounts for currency translation and pension fund adjustments – these are almost impossible to forecast and they are not a function of the normal business decision making process. For these reasons, there is little value in attempting to incorporate them into a financial statement model. In addition to the projected monetary values, percentages of sales revenue are included to facilitate common sizing and easier comparison of the results for each of the forecast periods.

Screenshot 9.3

	A	B	C	D	E	F	G	H	I
1	Omicron Design Company Limited								
2	**Statement of comprehensive income**								
3					period ending 31st December				
4			2017			2018		2019	
5		£000's	%		£000's	%		£000's	%
6	Sales revenue	144,000	100.0%		146,000	100.0%		147,000	100.0%
7	Cost of sales	(95,360)	(66.2%)		(96,218)	(65.9%)		(97,210)	(66.1%)
8	Gross profit	48,640	33.8%		49,782	34.1%		49,790	33.9%
9									
10	Administrative expenses	(31,750)	(22.0%)		(33,000)	(22.6%)		(34,000)	(23.1%)
11	Depreciation	(4,000)	(2.8%)		(4,500)	(3.1%)		(5,000)	(3.4%)
12	**Operating profit**	**12,890**	**9.0%**		**12,282**	**8.4%**		**10,790**	**7.3%**
13									
14	Finance costs	(700)	(0.5%)		(600)	(0.4%)		(500)	(0.3%)
15	Profit before tax	12,190	**8.5%**		11,682	**8.0%**		10,290	**7.0%**
16									
17	Taxation	(2,682)	(1.9%)		(2,570)	(1.8%)		(2,264)	(1.5%)
18	**Profit for the year**	**9,508**	**6.6%**		**9,112**	**6.2%**		**8,026**	**5.5%**
19									

The formulae used to generate the income statement are shown below – the illustration is for 2017, but the same approach is taken for 2018 and 2019.

The CONCATENATE text function is used in cell B3 to generate a conditional text header that changes the period ending details, dependent on the values assigned in the INPUT sheet for cell B3.

Note that administrative expenses include the profit or loss on any asset disposal.

The IFERROR function is used in column C to prevent the display of error messages in the event that missing input assumptions produce a division error: #DIV/o!

Screenshot 9.4

	A	B	C
1	=INPUT!B2		
2	**Statement of comprehensive income**		
3		=CONCATENATE("period ending ",INPUT!B3)	
4		=INPUT!C4	
5		£000's	%
6	Sales revenue	=INPUT!C6	=IFERROR(B6/B$6,0)
7	Cost of sales	=-ROUND(INPUT!C6*INPUT!C7+INPUT!C8,0)	=IFERROR(B7/B$6,0)
8	Gross profit	=B6+B7	=IFERROR(B8/B$6,0)
9			
10	Administrative expenses	=-INPUT!C9+INPUT!C15-INPUT!C14+INPUT!C18	=IFERROR(B10/B$6,0)
11	Depreciation	=-INPUT!C17	=IFERROR(B11/B$6,0)
12	**Operating profit**	**=B8+B10+B11**	**=IFERROR(B12/B$6,0)**
13			
14	Finance costs	=-INPUT!C27	=IFERROR(B14/B$6,0)
15	Profit before tax	=B12+B14	**=IFERROR(B15/B$6,0)**
16			
17	Taxation	=-ROUND(B15*INPUT!C10,0)	=IFERROR(B17/B$6,0)
18	**Profit for the year**	**=B15+B17**	**=IFERROR(B18/B$6,0)**
19			

The balance sheet forecast

The Financial Statement Forecasting Model produces a columnar format statement of financial position (balance sheet) and a supporting statement of changes in equity, as well as analysis notes for property, plant and equipment, and borrowing. Comparative figures are included for the prior year actual position based on the input assumptions in column B of the INPUT sheet.

Screenshot 9.5

	A	B	C	D	E	F	G	H
1	Omicron Design Company Limited							
2	**Statement of financial position**							
3	£000's omitted					as at 31st December		
4	2016			2017		2018		2019
5			**Non current assets**					
6	35,300		Property, plant and equipment	36,800		38,300		39,300
7	35,300			36,800		38,300		39,300
8			**Current assets**					
9	8,619		Inventories	9,027		7,794		8,659
10	29,384		Trade receivables	28,011		28,000		26,178
11	3,470		Cash and cash equivalents	5,508		7,164		8,059
12	41,473			42,546		42,958		42,896
13			**Current liabilities**					
14	(5,516)		Trade and other payables	(5,381)		(5,196)		(5,195)
15	(2,000)		Borrowings	(2,000)		(2,000)		(2,000)
16	(400)		Current tax liability	(590)		(565)		(498)
17	(7,916)			(7,971)		(7,761)		(7,693)
18								
19	33,557		**Net current assets**	34,575		35,197		35,203
20								
21			**Non-current liabilities**					
22	(11,000)		Borrowings	(9,000)		(7,000)		(5,000)
23	(350)		Deferred tax and other provisions	(360)		(370)		(350)
24	57,507		**Net assets**	62,015		66,127		69,153
25								
26	10,000		Share capital	10,000		10,000		10,000
27	1,650		Reserves	1,650		1,650		1,650
28	45,857		Retained earnings	50,365		54,477		57,503
29	57,507		**Shareholders' equity**	62,015		66,127		69,153
30								

Screenshot 9.6

		Share capital		Revaluation reserve		Retained earnings		Total
Statement of changes in shareholders' equity								
£000's omitted								
31st December 2016		10,000		1,650		45,857		57,507
Dividend payments						(5,000)		(5,000)
Profit for the year						9,508		9,508
31st December 2017		**10,000**		**1,650**		**50,365**		**62,015**
Dividend payments						(5,000)		(5,000)
Profit for the year						9,112		9,112
31st December 2018		**10,000**		**1,650**		**54,477**		**66,127**
Dividend payments						(5,000)		(5,000)
Profit for the year						8,026		8,026
31st December 2019		**10,000**		**1,650**		**57,503**		**69,153**

Screenshot 9.7

	31st December		
	2017	2018	2019
Property, plant and equipment			
£000's omitted			
Cost			
Opening balance	72,500	76,000	82,000
Additions	6,000	6,000	6,000
Disposals	(2,500)		
Closing balance	**76,000**	**82,000**	**88,000**
Accumulated depreciation			
Opening balance	37,200	39,200	43,700
Depreciation for the year	4,000	4,500	5,000
Disposals	(2,000)		
Closing balance	**39,200**	**43,700**	**48,700**
Carrying value	**36,800**	**38,300**	**39,300**

Screenshot 9.8

B	C	D	E	F	G	H
67						
68	**Borrowing**					
69	£000's omitted			31st December		
70		2017		2018		2019
71	Opening balance	13,000		11,000		9,000
72	New borrowing					
73	Repayments	(2,000)		(2,000)		(2,000)
74	**Closing balance**	**11,000**		**9,000**		**7,000**
75						
76	Current borrowing	2,000		2,000		2,000
77	Non-current borrowing	9,000		7,000		5,000
78						

The formulae used to generate the statement of financial position, statement of changes in equity and the associated notes are shown in Screenshot 9.9.

Screenshot 9.9

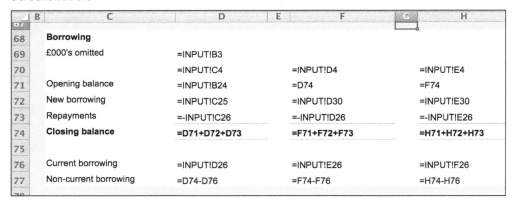

B	C	D	E	F	G	H
67						
68	Borrowing					
69	£000's omitted	=INPUT!B3				
70		=INPUT!C4		=INPUT!D4		=INPUT!E4
71	Opening balance	=INPUT!B24		=D74		=F74
72	New borrowing	=INPUT!C25		=INPUT!D30		=INPUT!E30
73	Repayments	=-INPUT!C26		=-INPUT!D26		=-INPUT!E26
74	Closing balance	=D71+D72+D73		=F71+F72+F73		=H71+H72+H73
75						
76	Current borrowing	=INPUT!D26		=INPUT!E26		=INPUT!F26
77	Non-current borrowing	=D74-D76		=F74-F76		=H74-H76

The borrowing analysis is generated from the input assumptions in rows 24 to 27 of the INPUT sheet, including that in cell F26 representing the part of the borrowing payable within 12 months of the end of the third year forecast. This is used to classify the appropriate element of borrowing as a current liability.

Screenshot 9.10

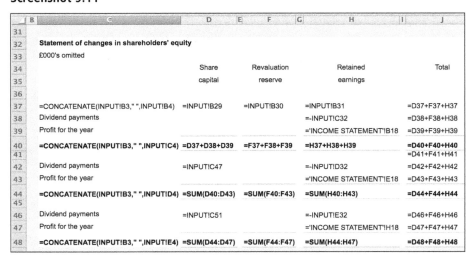

The assumptions for the property, plant and equipment analysis are taken from the non-current asset section of the INPUT sheet in rows 12 to 18.

Screenshot 9.11

	B	C	D	E	F	G	H	I	J
31									
32	Statement of changes in shareholders' equity								
33	£000's omitted								
34			Share		Revaluation		Retained		Total
35			capital		reserve		earnings		
36									
37	=CONCATENATE(INPUT!B3," ",INPUT!B4)		=INPUT!B29		=INPUT!B30		=INPUT!B31		=D37+F37+H37
38	Dividend payments						=-INPUT!C32		=D38+F38+H38
39	Profit for the year						='INCOME STATEMENT'!B18		=D39+F39+H39
40	=CONCATENATE(INPUT!B3," ",INPUT!C4)		=D37+D38+D39		=F37+F38+F39		=H37+H38+H39		=D40+F40+H40
41									=D41+F41+H41
42	Dividend payments		=INPUT!C47				=-INPUT!D32		=D42+F42+H42
43	Profit for the year						='INCOME STATEMENT'!E18		=D43+F43+H43
44	=CONCATENATE(INPUT!B3," ",INPUT!D4)		=SUM(D40:D43)		=SUM(F40:F43)		=SUM(H40:H43)		=D44+F44+H44
45									
46	Dividend payments		=INPUT!C51				=-INPUT!E32		=D46+F46+H46
47	Profit for the year						='INCOME STATEMENT'!H18		=D47+F47+H47
48	=CONCATENATE(INPUT!B3," ",INPUT!E4)		=SUM(D44:D47)		=SUM(F44:F47)		=SUM(H44:H47)		=D48+F48+H48

The profit for each of the years of the forecast is from the INCOME STATEMENT – all other assumptions are taken from the INPUT sheet. The CONCATENATE function has been used to provide dynamic text labelling for the statement.

The formulae shown in column A of the balance sheet are used to generate the previous year's balance sheet – these are taken from the assumptions in column B of the INPUT worksheet.

Screenshot 9.12

	A	B	C	D	E
1	=INPUT!B2				
2	Statement of financial position				
3	£000's omitted				
4	=INPUT!B4			=INPUT!C4	
5			Non current assets		
6	=INPUT!B12-INPUT!B16		Property, plant and equipment	=D66	
7	=A6			=D6	
8			Current assets		
9	=INPUT!B20		Inventories	=ROUND(INPUT!C6*INPUT!C7*INPUT!C20/365,0)	
10	=INPUT!B21		Trade receivables	=ROUND(INPUT!C6*INPUT!C21/365,0)	
11	=A12-A9-A10		Cash and cash equivalents	=D12-D9-D10	
12	=A19-A17			=D19-D17	
13			Current liabilities		
14	=-INPUT!B22		Trade and other payables	=-ROUND(INPUT!C6*INPUT!C7*INPUT!C22/365,0)	
15	=-INPUT!C26		Borrowings	=-D76	
16	=-INPUT!B34		Current tax liability	=ROUND('INCOME STATEMENT'!B17*INPUT!C35,0)	
17	=SUM(A14:A16)			=SUM(D14:D16)	
18					
19	=A24-A23-A22-A7		Net current assets	=D24-D23-D22-D7	
20					
21			Non-current liabilities		
22	=-INPUT!B24+INPUT!C26		Borrowings	=-D77	
23	=-INPUT!B36		Deferred tax and other provisions	=-INPUT!C36	
24	=A29		Net assets	=D29	
25					
26	=INPUT!B29		Share capital	=D40	
27	=INPUT!B30		Reserves	=F40	
28	=INPUT!B31		Retained earnings	=H40	
29	=SUM(A26:A28)		Shareholders' equity	=SUM(D26:D28)	

The formulae for the first year of the forecast period are shown above. The formulae for the second and third years follow the same approach.

The balance sheet values for non-current assets are taken from the property, plant and equipment section of the model in rows 51 to 66.

The forecast values for inventories, receivables and trade payables are calculated in the same way as they were for the cash flow model in Chapter 6. This allows the forecast model to establish a dynamic link between sales revenue and the level of inventory and trade credit needed to support it by using working capital ratios as input assumptions on the INPUT sheet:

- days' sales in inventory (DSI),

- days' sales outstanding (DSO) and

- days' purchases outstanding (DPO).

The balance sheet values for borrowings are taken from the borrowings section of the model in rows 68 to 77, including the split between the current liability portion and the non-current liability portion.

The current tax liability is calculated based on the profit on tax calculated in the income statement and the assumption for the percentage of tax unpaid at the balance sheet date, entered as an assumption in row 35 of the INPUT sheet.

Deferred tax and other provisions are entered as a single assumption in row 36 of the INPUT sheet.

The forecast values for shareholders' equity are taken from the statement of changes in shareholders' equity statement in rows 32 to 48.

At this stage cash and cash equivalents is the only value missing from the forecast. Since all other values are known, the cash figure can be deduced from those values. The accounting equation dictates that the net asset value should always be equal to shareholders' equity so the value in D24 must be equal to that in D29 (and the same will, of course, apply to the forecast balance sheet for year 2 and 3). Since the value for non-current assets and non-current liabilities is known, we can calculate the value for net current assets.

The cash flow statement forecast

Screenshot 9.13

	A	B	C	D	E	F	G
1	Omicron Design Company Limited						
2	**Statement of cash flows**						
3	£000's omitted			period ending 31st December			
4			2017		2018		2019
5							
6	Operating profit		12,890		12,282		10,790
7	Profit / loss on disposal of assets		(250)				
8	Depreciation		4,000		4,500		5,000
9	Interest paid		(700)		(600)		(500)
10	Tax paid		(2,492)		(2,595)		(2,331)
11			13,448		13,587		12,959
12							
13	(Increase)/decrease in inventory		(408)		1,233		(865)
14	(Increase)/decrease in receivables		1,373		11		1,822
15	(Decrease)/increase in trade and other payables		(135)		(185)		(1)
16	(Decrease)/increase in provisions		10		10		(20)
17	**Net cash generated from operating activities**		**14,288**		**14,656**		**13,895**
18							
19	Purchase of plant and equipment		(6,000)		(6,000)		(6,000)
20	Proceeds from sale of assets		750				
21	**Net cash used in investing activities**		**(5,250)**		**(6,000)**		**(6,000)**
22							
23	Repayment of borrowings		(2,000)		(2,000)		(2,000)
24	Dividend payments		(5,000)		(5,000)		(5,000)
25	**Net cash used in financing activities**		**(7,000)**		**(7,000)**		**(7,000)**
26							
27	**Net change in cash and cash equivalents**		**2,038**		**1,656**		**895**
28							
29	Cash and cash equivalents at start of the year		3,470		5,508		7,164
30	**Cash and cash equivalents at end of the year**		**5,508**		**7,164**		**8,059**

The Financial Statement Forecasting Model produces a statement of cash flows using the indirect method to present the operating cash flow section. The formulae to produce the statement for year 1 of the forecast are shown in Screenshot 9.14. Years 2 and 3 are calculated in the same way.

Screenshot 9.14

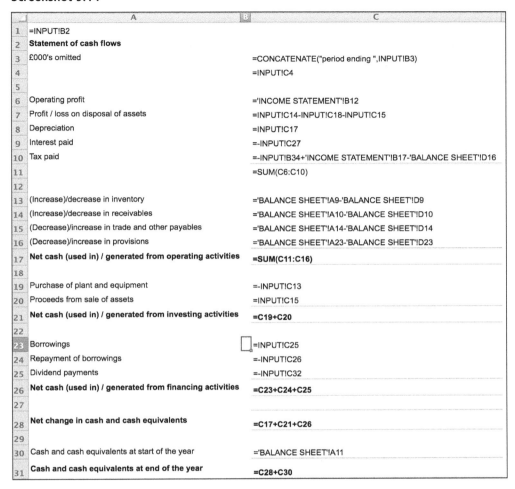

	A	B	C
1	=INPUT!B2		
2	**Statement of cash flows**		
3	£000's omitted		=CONCATENATE("period ending ",INPUT!B3)
4			=INPUT!C4
5			
6	Operating profit		='INCOME STATEMENT'!B12
7	Profit / loss on disposal of assets		=INPUT!C14-INPUT!C18-INPUT!C15
8	Depreciation		=INPUT!C17
9	Interest paid		=-INPUT!C27
10	Tax paid		=-INPUT!B34+'INCOME STATEMENT'!B17-'BALANCE SHEET'!D16
11			=SUM(C6:C10)
12			
13	(Increase)/decrease in inventory		='BALANCE SHEET'!A9-'BALANCE SHEET'!D9
14	(Increase)/decrease in receivables		='BALANCE SHEET'!A10-'BALANCE SHEET'!D10
15	(Decrease)/increase in trade and other payables		='BALANCE SHEET'!A14-'BALANCE SHEET'!D14
16	(Decrease)/increase in provisions		='BALANCE SHEET'!A23-'BALANCE SHEET'!D23
17	**Net cash (used in) / generated from operating activities**		**=SUM(C11:C16)**
18			
19	Purchase of plant and equipment		=-INPUT!C13
20	Proceeds from sale of assets		=INPUT!C15
21	**Net cash (used in) / generated from investing activities**		**=C19+C20**
22			
23	Borrowings		=INPUT!C25
24	Repayment of borrowings		=-INPUT!C26
25	Dividend payments		=-INPUT!C32
26	**Net cash (used in) / generated from financing activities**		**=C23+C24+C25**
27			
28	**Net change in cash and cash equivalents**		**=C17+C21+C26**
29			
30	Cash and cash equivalents at start of the year		='BALANCE SHEET'!A11
31	**Cash and cash equivalents at end of the year**		**=C28+C30**

The executive summary

The executive summary presents comparative key numbers from the three financial statements and calculates profitability, capital structure and cash flow ratios.

Screenshot 9.15

	A	B	C	D	E	F
1	Omicron Design Company Limited					
2	**Executive summary**					
3	£000's omitted					
4				FORECAST		
5		2017		2018		2019
6	**Financial performance**					
7	Sales revenue	144,000		146,000		147,000
8	Sales revenue growth			1.4%		0.7%
9						
10	Gross profit	48,640		49,782		49,790
11	Gross profit %	33.8%		34.1%		33.9%
12						
13	EBITDA	16,890		16,782		15,790
14	EBITDA % on sales revenue	11.7%		11.5%		10.7%
15						
16	Operating profit	12,890		12,282		10,790
17	Profit margin	9.0%		8.4%		7.3%
18						
19	Cash flow	2,038		1,656		895
20	Cash at year-end	5,508		7,164		8,059
21						
22	**Profitability ratios**					
23	Return on Net Assets	17.6%		16.3%		14.1%
24	Net asset turnover	1.96		1.93		1.92
25						
26	Return on Equity	15.3%		13.8%		11.6%
27						
28	**Capital structure and risk ratios**					
29	Gearing ratio	15.0%		11.9%		9.1%
30	Interest cover	18.41		20.47		21.58
31						
32	**Cash flow ratios**					
33	Operating cash flow ratio	1.8		1.9		1.8
34	Cash flow margin ratio	9.9%		10.0%		9.5%
35	Cash flow to debt ratio	84.2%		99.3%		109.5%

The formulae to generate the executive summary are shown in Screenshot 9.16 for the first year of the forecast. The executive summary for years 2 and 3 are calculated in a similar manner, with the addition of the formula in D8 to calculate sales growth percentage.

Screenshot 9.16

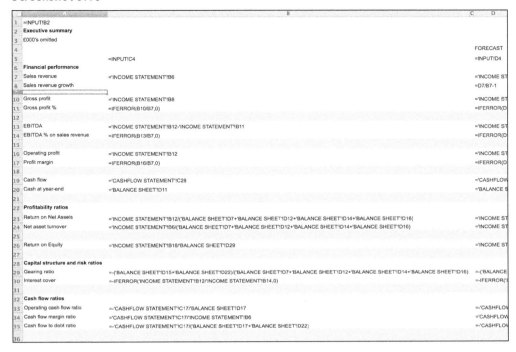

By using a small number of key business driver assumptions to produce a full set of financial statement forecasts, it is possible to quickly update the forecasts and test the impact of various kinds of risk events on the most important measures of financial performance and financial strength. The great benefit of this approach is in testing and observing the impact of different kinds of risks which provides real insights in to exactly how shareholder value is created and the kind of changes in input that produce the greatest value in the output.

Chapter 10

Model 7:
Business Valuation

There are few, if any, more contentious areas of finance than business valuation. Despite the existence of hundreds of books and scholarly articles on the subject, we still tend to be left with the question of whether business valuation is really an art or a science. It certainly provokes strong sentiment on the part of both prospective buyers and sellers in transactions where companies change hands.

There are two broad approaches to valuing businesses: those that focus on the value of the assets being sold and those that base the valuation on the income generated by those assets. The most common practical challenge is to place a value on the shares that need to be sold by the existing shareholders to the putative shareholders in order to achieve the change in ownership. The Business Valuation Model uses a cash flow (income based) approach to calculating a value for the shares being sold – a common method referred to as Shareholder Value Analysis (SVA).

The Business Valuation Model

- **Users:** Investment analysts, bank analysts, financial analysts, chief financial officers or finance directors would typically use this financial model to value a business.

- **Purpose:** The model uses free cash flow (FCF) drivers to value a business using the Shareholder Value Added (SVA) method, based on calculating the present value of all future FCF generated by the business.

- **Outputs:** The output is in the form of an SVA business valuation.

- **Inputs:** The illustration is based on a company in which growth is to be generated by the launch of a new product. There are detailed input assumptions to support the growth prediction for the new product and other assumptions for the established part of the business.

- **Calculations:** The calculations for the SVA model are incorporated into the outputs for the valuation.

- **Design:** Key driver assumptions are entered into the two INPUT sheets. A detailed EBITDA ANALYSIS gives a detailed breakdown of how profit is driven by new and existing products. The SVA MODEL is a business valuation that can be used for the purposes of testing the valuation and presenting it as the basis for a discussion about the valuation and the key risk factors.

Topic refresher – business valuation

Who needs to value businesses and why? CEOs and senior managers of today's listed companies are acutely aware of the need to maintain and build shareholder value. They need a means of calculating their own company's valuation to assess whether the stock market is placing a realistic value on the company's shares. They may also use the same business valuation tools to identify companies that are undervalued by the stock market and represent potential acquisition targets.

Investment analysts in banks and advisory firms constantly produce and update their own valuations of listed companies in order to advise their clients on which shares are currently over- or undervalued by various stock markets, and whether their shares should be bought, sold or held.

Unlisted companies need to establish a value for the business before deciding on a price at which to offer the shares in an initial public offering (IPO) on a stock market.

Similarly, a value will need to be established if the company is going to be sold directly to a new owner. The real value of a business is, of course, ultimately reflected in what the buyer is prepared to pay to acquire the company and what the seller is prepared to accept. Even the best business valuation tools will only provide guidance on the price range in which such a negotiation might take place.

Perhaps one of the most common contexts in which an unlisted firm needs to establish a value for the business is when it is seeking new equity investment – often from venture capital investors at the point at which a new product is being developed for launch, or is poised for a phase of high sales growth. In this case, the valuation model may form part of the business plan being presented to the prospective investors and will provide the basis of negotiations about the investment required and the proportion of the total equity this might buy.

Asset-based valuation models focus on the net tangible assets of a business as the basis for a valuation, though different figures are produced – depending on the way in which the assets and liabilities are valued. A valuation may be based on the balance sheet value of the company's net assets, in which case the valuation will be influenced by the asset valuation policy basis chosen by the company. If assets have been valued on the basis of their historical cost, they will be shown in the balance sheet at their original cost minus the accumulated depreciation charged against the asset. If the company has adopted a revaluation basis, the assets may at some point have been adjusted to fair market value and subsequently depreciated from that basis.

Alternatively, adjustments may be made in the valuation to bring the balance sheet asset values into line with their replacement cost, or their net realisable value. The latter approach will give a guide to the break-up value in the event of liquidating the company, and may represent the lowest price that may be acceptable to the sellers in the event of a sale. The stock market valuation of poorly performing companies may sometimes fall below their net realisable value, and this may present an opportunity for so-called asset strippers to acquire the company to be broken up.

Asset-based valuations may be useful to some extent for companies in which the ability to generate customer and shareholder value is heavily dependent on tangible physical assets: for example, property development firms. A major weakness in this approach is that it is focused on the value of those tangible assets at a particular date, and may not provide a real indication of the value that may be generated by these assets in future years. More critically, in digital age enterprises, like Google, Facebook and Airbnb, it is the intangible assets like customer relationships, brands, human talent and innovative software that drive customer and shareholder value. The way in which accounting concepts and rules are applied prevents the real value of these internally-generated intangibles being properly reflected in balance sheet asset values.

Modigliani and Miller argue that the real value of a business is a function of its earning power and the risks to the underlying assets of the business. There are a number of valuation methods that focus on company earnings.

The price/earnings (P/E) ratio is perhaps the most common of the earnings multiple methods and is based on the ratio of the market price of a share to its annual shareholder earnings (profit after interest and taxation) per share. P/E ratios for public companies are published in financial pages of newspapers and on financial websites. For private companies, a P/E ratio may be based on that of a quoted company in a similar industry sector, but the ratio may be reduced to reflect the greater risk involved investing in private companies because of, amongst other things, the difficulty in trading the shares. This method of calculating a value for an unquoted company in the absence of a stock market value is:

Business value = company's post tax profit × applicable P/E ratio

This simple, income-based approach may provide a useful rule of thumb guide to the value of a business, but ultimately relies on an arbitrary choice of multiple. Profit calculations are subject to accounting adjustments, some of which may be quite subjective, and may also be distorted by deliberate attempts to manipulate them.

The dividend valuation model is also an income-based valuation method, but in this case the valuation is based on expected future dividends rather than on earnings. The model implies that the fair value of a business is equal to the value of all the future dividends that a shareholder might expect to receive from those shares in the future. In this case, the value can be estimated by discounting expected future dividends in perpetuity to a present value at the shareholders' cost of capital. One version of this model assumes a constant rate of dividends in perpetuity, while another applies a constant growth rate to the dividends. This method has the advantage of using actual cash dividends expected to be paid rather than a subjective measure of profit. But not all companies pay dividends and this method takes no view of the company's future ability to create value. Shareholders' cost of capital may be difficult to establish and, in any event, may not be a true reflection of the risk in the company's underlying assets.

The Shareholder Value Added (SVA) method of business valuation

Modigliani and Miller argued that the value of a business should be measured by reference to the present value of all of its future cash flows (FCF), calculated as operating cash flows adjusted for changes in working capital and cash investment in the replacement and maintenance of plant and equipment. The shareholder value added (SVA) method of business valuation treats the purchase of a company as a capital investment and is based on the present value of future projected FCF. This method produces a price at which the shares in the company should be acquired. The discount rate used for the SVA calculation is the company's weighted average cost of capital (WACC). This is used on the basis that the market's own assessment is the best indicator of the inherent risk in the company and this is reflected in the cost of its equity and debt.

The valuation is then made as:

$$Company\ value\ =\ \frac{Projected\ free\ cash\ flows}{Company's\ WACC}$$

Three steps should be followed in the SVA valuation method:

1. Calculate the value of the company's operational assets based on the discounted present value of the projected future operational free cash flows.

2. Add the market value of any non-operational assets, like surplus cash, investments and any other assets that are not actively employed in the business. The sum of the value of operational assets and the value of non-operational assets represents the total value of the business assets – the so-called *enterprise value*.

3. Subtract from the enterprise value the market value (where it is known) of the company's debt. This, then, gives a valuation for the shareholders' equity.

The key shareholder value drivers

For the purposes of designing a financial model to apply the SVA method, the key drivers of shareholder value can be considered as the:

- **Sales growth rate**: Percentage growth in annual sales revenue.

- **Operating profit margin**: Expected earnings before interest and tax, depreciation and amortisation (EBITDA) as a percentage of sales revenue.

- **Tax rate**: The rate of tax on operating profit. This is a cash tax rate and ignores deferred taxation.

- **Incremental working capital investment (IWCI)**: The additional cash invested in working capital when sales revenue increases.

- **Replacement fixed capital investment (RFCI)**: The amount of investment needed to replace non-current assets that reach the end of their economic life. Ignoring inflation, it is often assumed that RFCI is equal to the annual depreciation charge for non-current assets.

- **Incremental fixed capital investment (IFCI)**: The investment each year in non-current assets in excess of the amount needed for the replacement of existing non-current assets.

- **The target company's cost of capital**: Used to discount cash flows to a net present value for the purpose of valuing the business. For listed companies, the company's weighted average cost of capital (WACC) is used as the discount factor.

- **Competitive advantage period**: Also referred to as the *value growth duration*, or the discrete period. This is the period during which the business is expected to achieve growth. When the SVA method is applied to value a business in a proposed acquisition, or when applied in attracting new investment to support a proposed growth strategy, the value growth duration is taken to be the period during which the strategy is executed and produces its full intended effect. In practice this often works out to be between three and five years.

- **Residual value**: The present value at the end of the competitive advantage period of all of the company's future free cash flows. It may be assumed that the annual FCF after the competitive advantage period will be a constant annual amount or, alternatively, it may be assumed that these cash flows will continue to grow.

Valuation of the operational assets

There are three steps to calculate the value of the operational assets:

1. Make a forecast of the free cash flows (FCF) for each year of the competitive advantage period:

Operating profit before interest and tax	a
Deduct the tax payable on the operating profit	(b)
Operating cash flow after tax	c
Add back depreciation, amortisation and impairment charges	d
Sub total	e
Adjust for:	
Incremental working capital investment	(f)
Replacement fixed capital investment	(g)
Incremental capital investment	(h)
FREE CASH FLOW	i

When valuing a businesses that is part of a group of companies, or in the case of an unlisted company, sometimes it may be necessary to make adjustments to operating profit for transactions not at arms-length. Examples of this might include: inter-group service charges and transfer prices at other than market rates; or senior management salaries significantly below, or in excess of, normal market rates.

In the absence of better information, current depreciation may be used as an approximation to the annual replacement fixed cost investment, assuming that the company has invested adequately to maintain the productive capacity of the business.

The tax rate applied to operating profit should be the actual cash tax rate payable and should exclude the effect of tax relief on interest costs and ignore the impact of deferred taxation.

2. Calculate the residual value based on the present value of all future FCF generated by the company's operational assets after the end of the competitive advantage period by

using one of the methods described below. This value is treated as a cash receipt in the final year of the competitive advantage period.

3. Discount the combined FCF using the company's WACC.

Calculating the residual value of the operational assets

The residual value, continuing value or terminal value (*TV*) represents the value of an annual free cash flow in perpetuity after the end of the competitive advantage period, the present value of which is treated as a cash receipt at the end of the final year of the competitive advantage period. It may be assumed that the annual free cash flows will be a constant annual amount, equal to the final year FCF of the competitive advantage period. In this case the terminal value is calculated by dividing the annual FCF for the first year after the end of the competitive advantage period:

$$TV = \frac{FCF_{n+1}}{r}$$

The Perpetuity Growth Model assumes that the free cash flows will continue growing at a constant rate (g) in perpetuity. In this case the projected FCF in the first year beyond the discrete period (*n*+1) is calculated by applying the growth rate to the FCF in the final year of the competitive advantage period. The terminal value is then calculated as:

$$TV = \frac{FCF_{n+1}}{r - g}$$

The terminal value at the end of the competitive advantage period should reflect the market value of the business at that point, However, an alternative approach to calculating the terminal value is to apply an appropriate multiple to the EBITDA for the final year of the competitive advantage period.

The appropriate multiple may be determined by an analysis of recent business sales transactions in the same, or a similar, industry. Alternatively, the current market value of a public company can be calculated by reference to its share price. By comparing this to the most recent annual EBTIDA for the same company, a multiple can be calculated that represents the current market value. The EBITDA multiple may be adjusted to reflect any difference in size between the company, subject to the capital investment appraisal, and the reference company – smaller companies generally attract a lower multiple for various reasons, including the somewhat greater perceived risk.

The Business Valuation Model

The illustrative example is of an unlisted pharmaceutical company that has developed a new therapeutic drug to treat Type 2 Diabetes. DMT2Z avoids some of the most significant adverse side effects of existing non-insulin therapies. The drug has been proven to be safe and effective and has been approved for use in the UK, Europe and the US. Additional investment is required to fund the completion of the expanded UK distribution facility that will be needed to handle the expected significant increase in business generated by the new drug. Further funding is also needed to finance the additional marketing and additional working capital. This additional investment is beyond the level that can be financed by the firm and so negotiations are taking place with private equity investors to buy a substantial stake in the company.

In this case a business valuation is required in order to agree the proportion of the firm's equity that will be attributed to the new private equity investors. The Business Valuation Model has been designed to be used for presenting a business plan and valuation to potential investors. For this reason, a very detailed set of basic assumptions has been used to build a detailed forecast of free cash flows generated by the new drug as it is launched and market share is built over five years. This will allow the valuation to be tested against specific identifiable risks in the forecast; for example, the expected future incidence and types of diabetes that might occur within the population. In addition to the very detailed forecast for the new drug, a broader based approach has been taken to forecasting the cash flows generated by the existing business that markets and distributes a number of other pharmaceutical products. Revenues in the existing business have stabilised and are expected to grow at significantly lower rates than the new diabetes drug. The company's most recent financial statements are shown below.

KAPPA PI THERAPUTICS

Income statement for year ending 31st December

£000's omitted	2017		2016	
Sales	211,000	100.0%	188,000	100.0%
Cost of goods sold	(70,685)	(33.5)%	(64,484)	(34.3)%
Gross margin	140,315	66.5%	123,516	65.7%
Distribution costs	(21,500)	(10.2)%	(19,100)	(10.2)%
Marketing costs	(21,000)	(10.0)%	(18,000)	(9.6)%
Gross profit	97,815	46.4%	86,416	46.0%

Royalty income	21,300	10.1%	18,700	9.9%
Contribution	119,115	56.5%	105,116	55.9%
Administrative expenses	(25,300)	(12.0)%	(23,800)	(12.7)%
Research and development	(18,500)	(8.8)%	(17,300)	(9.2)%
Depreciation	(7,200)	(3.4)%	(6,800)	(3.6)%
Operating profit	**68,115**	**32.3%**	**57,216**	**30.4%**
Finance costs	(3,000)	(1.4)%	(3,000)	(1.6)%
Profit before tax	65,115	30.9%	54,216	28.8%
Taxation	(13,023)	(6.2)%	(10,843)	(5.8)%
PROFIT AFTER TAX	**52,092**	**24.7%**	**43,373**	**23.1%**

KAPPA PI THERAPUTICS

Balance sheet as at 31st December

£000's omitted	2017	2016
Non-current assets		
Property, plant and equipment	231,600	221,800
	231,600	221,800
Current assets		
Inventories	37,306	32,779
Trade receivables	49,137	38,630
Cash and cash equivalents	15,356	5,248
	101,799	76,657
Current liabilities		
Trade and other payables	(9,683)	(8,833)

Net current assets	**92,116**	**67,824**
Non-current liabilities		
Borrowings	(50,000)	(50,000)
NET ASSETS	**273,716**	**239,624**
Share capital	100,000	100,000
Retained earnings	173,716	139,624
SHAREHOLDERS' EQUITY	**273,716**	**239,624**

KAPPA PI THERAPUTICS

Cash flow statement for year ending 31st December

£000's omitted	2015	2014
Operating profit	68,115	57,216
Depreciation	7,200	6,800
Interest paid	(3,000)	(3,000)
Tax paid	(13,023)	(10,843)
	59,292	50,173
(Increase)/decrease in inventories	(4,527)	(5,441)
(Increase)/decrease in receivables	(10,507)	(2,904)
(Decrease)/increase in payables	850	1,085
Net cash generated from operating activities	**45,108**	**42,913**
Purchase of plant and equipment	(17,000)	(15,000)
Net cash used in investing activities	**(17,000)**	**(15,000)**

Repayment of borrowings

Dividend payments	(18,000)	(15,000)
Net cash used in financing activities	**(18,000)**	**(15,000)**
NET CHANGE IN CASH AND CASH EQUIVALENTS	**10,108**	**12,913**
Cash and cash equivalents at start of the year	5,248	(7,665)
Cash and cash equivalents at end of the year	**15,356**	**5,248**

The Business Valuation Model comprises four worksheets:

- An input sheet for a detailed set of assumptions on which to base the operating cash flow forecast for DMT2Z, the new diabetes drug.

- An input sheet for the remaining assumptions about working capital, capital investment and other relevant information to generate the other cash flows generated by the existing business.

- A detailed EBITDA forecast analysis.

- A shareholder value analysis (SVA) in which the business value is calculated.

DMT2Z product margin assumptions

The assumptions on which the product margin for the new product are based can be found in the DMT2Z ASSUMPTIONS worksheet. They have been built up to a detailed level, tracing the sales volume forecast back to the most basic sales volume drivers. This approach has been taken so that the sales and margin forecast is completely transparent and can be adjusted for the purposes of testing the effects of various kinds of risks on the business valuation. Sales revenues and margins for the UK and Europe are based on the distribution of physical product, while the US business assumes that the product will be licensed to a third party for a royalty payment.

Other input assumptions

The new DMT2Z product is the main driver of growth for the business. The sales revenues and gross margin assumptions for all of the company's other mature products are entered into the INPUT worksheet. All of the other assumptions to complete the SVA analysis are included in this worksheet.

Screenshot 10.1

	A	B	C	D	E	F
1	**DMT2Z PRODUCT MARGIN ASSUMPTIONS**					
2		Year 1	Year 2	Year 3	Year 4	Year 5
3	**UK**					
4	Population - millions / % growth	65.0	0.8%	0.8%	0.8%	0.8%
5	Total incidence of diabetes %	6.5%	6.7%	7.0%	7.2%	7.5%
6	Diagnosed cases %	92.0%	93.0%	94.0%	95.0%	95.0%
7	Type 2 diabetes %	90.0%	90.0%	90.0%	90.0%	90.0%
8	Non insulin dependent %	90.0%	90.0%	90.0%	90.0%	90.0%
9	Market penetration %	2.0%	5.0%	10.0%	14.0%	18.0%
10	Wholesale price per month pack £	30.00	30.00	30.00	30.00	30.00
11	Cost per pack £	10.00	10.00	10.00	10.00	10.00
12	Distribution cost on revenue %	5.0%	5.0%	5.0%	5.0%	5.0%
13	Marketing costs on revenue %	15.0%	10.0%	7.0%	7.0%	5.0%
14						
15	**EU TERRITORIES**					
16	Population - millions / % growth	512.0	0.5%	0.5%	0.5%	0.5%
17	Total incidence of diabetes %	6.0%	6.2%	6.3%	6.4%	6.5%
18	Diagnosed cases %	94.0%	94.0%	94.0%	95.0%	95.0%
19	Type 2 diabetes %	88.0%	89.0%	90.0%	90.0%	90.0%
20	Non insulin dependent %	90.0%	90.0%	90.0%	90.0%	90.0%
21	Market penetration %	1.0%	3.0%	6.0%	10.0%	12.0%
22	Wholesale price per month pack €	35.00	35.00	35.00	35.00	35.00
23	Cost per pack €	12.00	12.00	12.00	12.00	12.00
24	Distribution cost on revenue %	10.0%	10.0%	10.0%	10.0%	10.0%
25	Marketing costs on revenue %	15.0%	10.0%	7.0%	7.0%	5.0%
26	**US**					
27	Population - millions / % growth	323.0	0.7%	0.7%	0.7%	0.7%
28	Total incidence of diabetes %	7.6%	7.8%	7.9%	8.0%	8.1%
29	Diagnosed cases %	90.0%	91.0%	92.0%	92.0%	92.0%
30	Type 2 diabetes %	95.0%	96.0%	96.0%	96.0%	97.0%
31	Non insulin dependent %	87.0%	87.0%	87.0%	87.0%	87.0%
32	Market penetration %	1.0%	2.0%	5.0%	7.0%	9.0%
33	Wholesale price per month pack $	40.0	40.0	40.0	40.0	40.0
34	Royalty on wholesale price %	30.0%	30.0%	30.0%	30.0%	30.0%
35						
36						

INPUT | DMT2Z ASSUMPTIONS | EBITDA ANALYSIS | SVA MODEL | +

Screenshot 10.2

	A	B	C	D	E	F	G
1	**KAPPA PI THERAPUTICS - BUSINESS VALUATION ASSUMPTIONS**						
2	£000's omitted		1	2	3	4	5
3	**Gross profit assumptions - current product range - UK**						
4	Sales revenue - £000's / growth %		58,000	5.0%	5.0%	5.0%	5.0%
5	Cost of goods sold % of revenue		32.8%	32.8%	32.8%	32.8%	32.8%
6	Distribution costs % of revenue		10.0%	10.0%	10.0%	10.0%	10.0%
7	Marketing costs % of revenue		10.0%	10.0%	10.0%	10.0%	10.0%
8	**Gross profit assumptions - current product range - EU**						
9	Sales revenue - €000's / growth %		164,000	5.0%	5.0%	5.0%	5.0%
10	Cost of goods sold % of revenue		34.3%	34.3%	34.3%	34.3%	34.3%
11	Distribution costs % of revenue		10.0%	10.0%	10.0%	10.0%	10.0%
12	Marketing costs % of revenue		10.0%	10.0%	10.0%	10.0%	10.0%
13	€ to £ exchange rate		1.10	1.10	1.10	1.10	1.10
14	**Gross profit assumptions - current product range - US**						
15	Royalty income - $000's / growth %		23,000	3.0%	2.0%	2.0%	2.0%
16	$ to £ exchange rate		1.30	1.30	1.30	1.30	1.30
17	Administrative expenses - £000's		27,000	30,000	33,000	36,000	40,000
18	Research and development - £000's		20,000	23,000	25,000	30,000	35,000
19	Effective cash tax rate - %		18.0%	18.0%	18.0%	18.0%	18.0%
20	**Working capital investment**						
21	Days' sales in inventory		165	165	165	165	165
22	Days' sales outstanding		70	70	70	70	70
23	Days' US royalty outstanding		90	90	90	90	90
24	Days' payable outstanding		50	50	50	50	50
25	Opening inventory - £000's	37,306					
26	Opening trade receivables - £000's	49,317					
27	Opening trade payables - £000's	9,683					
28	**Fixed capital investment**						
29	Replacement fixed capital investment - £000's		6,000	6,000	6,000	6,000	6,000
30	Incremental fixed capital investment - £000's		45,000	20,000	5,000		
31	**Other assumptions**						
32	Market value of non-operational assets - £000's	45,000					
33	Market value of debt - £000's	50,000					
34	Discount factor	12.0%					
35							

DMT2Z ASSUMPTIONS / INPUT / EBITDA ANALYSIS / SVA MODEL / +

EBITDA analysis

The assumptions from DMT2Z ASSUMPTIONS and INPUT worksheets are used in the EBITDA ANALYSIS worksheet to produce the detailed forecast of earnings before interest, taxation, depreciation and amortisation (EBITDA). That becomes the starting point for the operating cash flow forecast.

Screenshot 10.3

	A	B	C	D	E	F	G
1	KAPPA PI THERAPUTICS - DETAILED EBITDA ANALYSIS						
2	000's omitted	Year 1			Year 2		
3		DMT2Z	Other	Total	DMT2Z	Other	Total
4	UK						
5	Sales units DMT2Z	751.2			1,984.1		
6		£	£	£	£	£	£
7	Sales revenue	22,535	58,000	80,535	59,524	60,900	120,424
8	Cost of goods sold	(7,512)	(19,024)	(26,536)	(19,841)	(19,975)	(39,816)
9	Gross margin	15,023	38,976	53,999	39,682	40,925	80,607
10	Gross margin %	66.7%	67.2%	67.1%	66.7%	67.2%	66.9%
11	Distribution costs	(1,127)	(5,800)	(6,927)	(2,976)	(6,090)	(9,066)
12	Marketing costs	(3,380)	(5,800)	(9,180)	(5,952)	(6,090)	(12,042)
13	Gross profit	10,516	27,376	37,892	30,754	28,745	59,499
14	Gross profit %	46.7%	47.2%	47.1%	51.7%	47.2%	49.4%
15							
16	EU TERRITORIES						
17	Sales units DMT2Z	2,744.5			8,647.5		
18		£			£		
19	Sales revenue	87,323	149,091	236,414	275,148	156,545	431,693
20	Cost of goods sold	(29,939)	(51,138)	(81,078)	(94,336)	(53,695)	(148,031)
21	Gross margin	57,384	97,953	155,337	180,811	102,850	283,662
22	Gross margin %	65.7%	65.7%	65.7%	65.7%	65.7%	65.7%
23	Distribution costs	(8,732)	(14,909)	(23,641)	(27,515)	(15,655)	(43,169)
24	Marketing costs	(13,099)	(14,909)	(28,008)	(27,515)	(15,655)	(43,169)
25	Gross profit	35,553	68,135	103,688	125,782	71,541	197,323
26	Gross profit %	40.7%	45.7%	43.9%	45.7%	45.7%	45.7%
27							
28	US						
29	Sales units DMT2Z	2,191.2			4,627.7		
30		£			£		
31	Royalty income	20,226	17,692	37,919	42,718	18,223	60,941
32							
33	TOTAL						
34	Sales units DMT2Z	5,686.8			15,259.4		
35		£			£		
36	Sales revenue	109,858	207,091	316,949	334,671	217,445	552,117
37	Cost of goods sold	(37,451)	(70,162)	(107,613)	(114,178)	(73,670)	(187,848)

DMT2Z ASSUMPTIONS / INPUT / EBITDA ANALYSIS / SVA MODEL / +

Screenshot 10.4

	A	B	C	D	E	F	G
1	KAPPA PI THERAPUTICS - DETAILED EBITDA ANALYSIS						
2	000's omitted	Year 1			Year 2		
15							
16	EU TERRITORIES						
17	Sales units DMT2Z	2,744.5			8,647.5		
18		£			£		
19	Sales revenue	87,323	149,091	236,414	275,148	156,545	431,693
20	Cost of goods sold	(29,939)	(51,138)	(81,078)	(94,336)	(53,695)	(148,031)
21	Gross margin	57,384	97,953	155,337	180,811	102,850	283,662
22	Gross margin %	65.7%	65.7%	65.7%	65.7%	65.7%	65.7%
23	Distribution costs	(8,732)	(14,909)	(23,641)	(27,515)	(15,655)	(43,169)
24	Marketing costs	(13,099)	(14,909)	(28,008)	(27,515)	(15,655)	(43,169)
25	Gross profit	35,553	68,135	103,688	125,782	71,541	197,323
26	Gross profit %	40.7%	45.7%	43.9%	45.7%	45.7%	45.7%
27							
28	US						
29	Sales units DMT2Z	2,191.2			4,627.7		
30		£			£		
31	Royalty income	20,226	17,692	37,919	42,718	18,223	60,941
32							
33	TOTAL						
34	Sales units DMT2Z	5,686.8			15,259.4		
35		£			£		
36	Sales revenue	109,858	207,091	316,949	334,671	217,445	552,117
37	Cost of goods sold	(37,451)	(70,162)	(107,613)	(114,178)	(73,670)	(187,848)
38	Gross margin	72,407	136,929	209,336	220,494	143,775	364,269
39	Gross margin %	65.9%	66.1%	66.0%	65.9%	66.1%	66.0%
40	Distribution costs	(9,859)	(20,709)	(30,568)	(30,491)	(21,745)	(52,235)
41	Marketing costs	(16,479)	(20,709)	(37,188)	(33,467)	(21,745)	(55,212)
42	Gross profit	46,069	95,511	141,580	156,536	100,286	256,822
43	Gross profit %	41.9%	46.1%	44.7%	46.8%	46.1%	46.5%
44	Royalty income	20,226	17,692	37,919	42,718	18,223	60,941
45	Contribution	66,296	113,203	179,499	199,253	118,509	317,763
46		60.3%	54.7%	56.6%	59.5%	54.5%	57.6%
47	Administrative expenses			(27,000)			(30,000)
48	Research and development			(20,000)			(23,000)
49	EBITDA			132,499			264,763

DMT2Z ASSUMPTIONS / INPUT / EBITDA ANALYSIS / SVA MODEL / +

The formulae used to generate the EBITDA analysis are shown below. The illustration relates only to year 1, but the calculations are the same for each of the other years in the competitive advantage period (CAP).

Screenshot 10.5

	A	B (Year 1) — DMT2Z	C — Other	D — Total
1	KAPPA PI THERAPUTICS			
2	000's omitted			
3		Year 1	Other	Total
		DMT2Z		
4	UK			
5	Sales units DMT2Z	=DMT2Z ASSUMPTIONS!B4*1000*DMT2Z ASSUMPTIONS!B5*DMT2Z ASSUMPTIONS!B6*DMT2Z ASSUMPTIONS!B7*DMT2Z ASSUMPTIONS!B8*DMT2Z ASSUMPTIONS!B9*12		
6		£	£	£
7	Sales revenue	=B5*DMT2Z ASSUMPTIONS!B10	=INPUT!C4	=B7+C7
8	Cost of goods sold	=-B5*DMT2Z ASSUMPTIONS!B11	=-C7*INPUT!C5	=B8+C8
9	Gross margin	=B7+B8	=C7+C8	=D7+D8
10	Gross margin %	=IFERROR(B9/B7,0)	=IFERROR(C9/C7,0)	=IFERROR(D9/D7,0)
11	Distribution costs	=B7*DMT2Z ASSUMPTIONS!B12	=-C7*INPUT!C6	=B11+C11
12	Marketing costs	=B7*DMT2Z ASSUMPTIONS!B13	=-C7*INPUT!C7	=B12+C12
13	Gross profit	=B9+B11+B12	=C9+C11+C12	=D9+D11+D12
14	Gross profit %	=IFERROR(B13/B7,0)	=IFERROR(C13/C7,0)	=IFERROR(D13/D7,0)
15				
16	EU TERRITORIES			
17	Sales units DMT2Z	=DMT2Z ASSUMPTIONS!B16*1000*DMT2Z ASSUMPTIONS!B17*DMT2Z ASSUMPTIONS!B18*DMT2Z ASSUMPTIONS!B19*DMT2Z ASSUMPTIONS!B20*DMT2Z ASSUMPTIONS!B21*12		
18		£	£	£
19	Sales revenue	=B17*DMT2Z ASSUMPTIONS!B22/INPUT!C13	=INPUT!$C9/INPUT!C13	=B19+C19
20	Cost of goods sold	=-B17*DMT2Z ASSUMPTIONS!B23/INPUT!$C13	=-C19*INPUT!C10	=B20+C20
21	Gross margin	=B19+B20	=C19+C20	=D19+D20
22	Gross margin %	=IFERROR(B21/B19,0)	=IFERROR(C21/C19,0)	=IFERROR(D21/D19,0)
23	Distribution costs	=-B19*DMT2Z ASSUMPTIONS!B24	=-C19*INPUT!C11	=B23+C23
24	Marketing costs	=-B19*DMT2Z ASSUMPTIONS!B25	=-C19*INPUT!C12	=B24+C24
25	Gross profit	=B21+B23+B24	=C21+C23+C24	=D21+D23+D24
26	Gross profit %	=IFERROR(B25/B19,0)	=IFERROR(C25/C19,0)	=IFERROR(D25/D19,0)
27				
28	US			
29	Sales units DMT2Z	=DMT2Z ASSUMPTIONS!B27*1000*DMT2Z ASSUMPTIONS!B28*DMT2Z ASSUMPTIONS!B29*DMT2Z ASSUMPTIONS!B30*DMT2Z ASSUMPTIONS!B31*DMT2Z ASSUMPTIONS!B32*12		
30		£	£	£
31	Royalty income	=B29*DMT2Z ASSUMPTIONS!B33*DMT2Z ASSUMPTIONS!B34/INPUT!C16	=INPUT!C15/INPUT!C16	=B31+C31

Screenshot 10.6

	A	B	C	D
1	**KAPPA PI THERAPUTICS**			
2	000's omitted	Year 1		
35		£		
36	Sales revenue	=B7+B19	=C7+C19	=D7+D19
37	Cost of goods sold	=B8+B20	=C8+C20	=D8+D20
38	Gross margin	=B36+B37	=C36+C37	=D36+D37
39	Gross margin %	=IFERROR(B38/B36,0)	=IFERROR(C38/C36,0)	=IFERROR(D38/D36,0)
40	Distribution costs	=B11+B23	=C11+C23	=D11+D23
41	Marketing costs	=B12+B24	=C12+C24	=D12+D24
42	Gross profit	=B38+B40+B41	=C38+C40+C41	=D38+D40+D41
43	Gross profit %	=IFERROR(B42/B36,0)	=IFERROR(C42/C36,0)	=IFERROR(D42/D36,0)
44	Royalty income	=B31	=C31	=D31
45	**Contribution**	**=B42+B44**	**=C42+C44**	**=D42+D44**
46		=IFERROR(B45/B36,0)	=IFERROR(C45/C36,0)	=IFERROR(D45/D36,0)
47	Administrative expenses			=-INPUT!C17
48	Research and development			=-INPUT!C18
49	**EBITDA**			**=D45+D47+D48**
50				=IFERROR(D49/D36,0)

SVA model

The SVA model uses the total EBITDA calculation from the EBITDA ANALYSIS and other assumptions from the INPUT worksheet to produce the shareholder value added valuation for the company. The SVA MODEL worksheet is shown below.

Screenshot 10.7

	A	B	C	D	E	F	G
1	KAPPA PI THERAPUTICS - SHAREHOLDER VALUE ANALYSIS						
2	£000's omitted	NPV	1	2	3	4	5
3	EBITDA		132,499	264,763	522,114	798,424	1,017,923
4	Tax paid on EBITDA		(23,850)	(47,657)	(93,980)	(143,716)	(183,226)
5	Operating cash flow		108,649	217,105	428,133	654,708	834,696
6							
7	Inventory		48,647	84,918	142,141	216,195	261,891
8	Receivables		70,135	120,912	208,810	312,487	382,079
9	Payables		(14,742)	(25,733)	(43,073)	(65,514)	(79,361)
10	Working capital		104,040	180,097	307,879	463,168	564,609
11	Incremental working capital		(27,100)	(76,057)	(127,782)	(155,290)	(101,440)
12							
13	Replacement capital investment		(6,000)	(6,000)	(6,000)	(6,000)	(6,000)
14	Incremental capital investment		(45,000)	(20,000)	(5,000)	0	0
15	Total fixed capital investment		(51,000)	(26,000)	(11,000)	(6,000)	(6,000)
16							
17	FREE CASH FLOWS	1,051,187	30,549	115,049	289,351	493,418	727,256
18							
19	Residual value	3,918,539	0	0	0	0	6,905,804
20							
21	VALUE OF OPERATIONAL ASSETS	4,969,726					
22							
23	Market value of non-operational assets	45,000					
24							
25	ENTERPRISE VALUE OF BUSINESS	5,014,726					
26							
27	Market value of debt	(50,000)					
28							
29	SHAREHOLDER VALUE ADDED	4,964,726					
30							
31							
32							
33							

DMT2Z ASSUMPTIONS / INPUT / EBITDA ANALYSIS / SVA MODEL / +

The worksheet formulae used to calculate free cash flows generated by the operational assets in the first two years of the CAP are shown below. For clarity, column B has been hidden. The free cash flows generated by operational assets for years 3 to 5 of the CAP are calculated in the same manner as those in year 2 in the worksheet extract below.

Screenshot 10.8

	A	C	D
1	KAPPA PI THERAPUTICS - SHAREHOLDER VALUE ANALYSIS		
2	£000's omitted	1	2
3	EBITDA	='EBITDA ANALYSIS'!D49	='EBITDA ANALYSIS'!G49
4	Tax paid on EBITDA	=-C3*INPUT!$C19	=-D3*INPUT!$C19
5	Operating cash flow	=C3+C4	=D3+D4
6			
7	Inventory	=-INPUT!C21/365*'EBITDA ANALYSIS'!D37	=-INPUT!D21/365*'EBITDA ANALYSIS'!G37
8	Receivables	=INPUT!C22/365*'EBITDA ANALYSIS'!D36+INPUT!C23/365*'EBITDA ANALYSIS'!D44	=INPUT!D22/365*'EBITDA ANALYSIS'!G36+INPUT!D23/365*'EBITDA ANALYSIS'!G44
9	Payables	=INPUT!C24/365*'EBITDA ANALYSIS'!D37	=INPUT!D24/365*'EBITDA ANALYSIS'!G37
10	Working capital	=C7+C8+C9	=D7+D8+D9
11	Incremental working capital	=(INPUT!B25+INPUT!B26-INPUT!B27)-C10	=C10-D10
12			
13	Replacement capital investment	=-INPUT!C29	=-INPUT!D29
14	Incremental capital investment	=-INPUT!C30	=-INPUT!D30
15	Total fixed capital investment	=C13+C14	=D13+D14
16			
17	FREE CASH FLOWS	=C5+C11+C15	=D5+D11+D15
18			

For each year of the CAP, the EBITDA figure is taken from the EBITDA ANALYSIS worksheet, and the cash tax percentage payable on EBITDA is taken from the INPUT worksheet, to be applied against the EBITDA figure.

For each year of the CAP the forecast, values for inventories, receivables and trade payables are calculated in the same way as they were for the cash flow model in Chapter 6 and the financial statement forecast model in Chapter 9. This allows the forecast model to establish a dynamic link between sales revenue from the EBITDA ANALYSIS worksheet and the level of inventory and trade credit needed to support it – by using working capital ratios as input assumptions on the INPUT sheet:

- Days' sales in inventory (DSI),
- days' sales outstanding (DSO), and
- days' purchases outstanding (DPO).

The total working capital investment is then calculated in row 10 of the SVA MODEL, and the relevant figure for the free cash flow calculation is the annual increase or decrease in working capital investment. For the first year of the CAP the change in working capital investment is calculated by reference to the opening working capital assumptions in rows 25 to 27 of the INPUT worksheet, while in the remaining years of the CAP the increase or decrease is calculated by reference to the previous year of the CAP. The fixed capital assumptions are taken directly from the INPUT worksheet.

The worksheet formulae for the remainder of the components for the SVA calculation are shown below – for clarity, columns C to F have been hidden.

Screenshot 10.9

	A	B	G
1	KAPPA PI THERAPUTICS - SHAREHOLDER VALUE ANALYSIS		
2	£000's omitted	NPV	5
16			
17	FREE CASH FLOWS	=NPV(INPUT!B$34,'SVA MODEL (2)'!C17:G17)	=G5+G11+G15
18			
19	Residual value	=NPV(INPUT!B$34,'SVA MODEL (2)'!C19:G19)	=(G5+G13)/INPUT!B34
20			
21	VALUE OF OPERATIONAL ASSETS	=B17+B19	
22			
23	Market value of non-operational assets	=INPUT!B32	
24			
25	ENTERPRISE VALUE OF BUSINESS	=B21+B23	
26			
27	Market value of debt	=-INPUT!B33	
28			
29	SHAREHOLDER VALUE ADDED	=B25+B27	

Residual value, representing the value of the business at the end of year 5, has been calculated using the perpetuity method – assuming a constant rate of free cash flow based on year 5. The formula in G19 of the SVA MODEL worksheet divides the sum of the operating cash flow (in G5 of the worksheet) and the replacement capital investment (in G13 of the worksheet) by the discount rate (taken from cell B34 of the INPUT worksheet). Since sales revenue is implicitly assumed to be constant, it may be assumed that there will be no further change in the level of working capital needed to support revenue and so no increase or decrease in the free cash flow to fund it. Note that cells C19 to F19 are populated with zeros rather than leaving cells blank. This is to ensure that the Excel NPV function treats the residual value in cell G19 as a year 5 cash flow. Were C19 to F19 left blank, the NPV function would treat the amount in cell G19 as a year 1 cash flow.

The market value of non-operational assets and the market value of debt are both values that have been taken directly from the INPUT worksheet.

The obvious value in this kind of business valuation model is that it provides a guide for the price that might be appropriate in any one of the circumstances discussed at the beginning of the chapter. In practice, the real benefit of this kind of dynamic financial model is that by spending time testing the impact of various kinds of risks on the ultimate SVA figure, it is possible to build useful insights into how value is driven through the business, as well as ascertaining the company's potential to improve shareholder value. It may also be helpful in informing the focus of the due diligence process.

The perpetuity growth method has been used for the purpose of illustrating its application in calculating the terminal value at the end of the five-year competitive advantage period. In practice, it may be more likely that a simpler EBITDA multiple would be used. The model can be easily adapted to make this change.

9 780857 195739